Desiree opens her heart authentically once again, proving that true love always prevails. The message I most cherish from this book is to remember to trust the process. It might not always be pretty, but it will be worth it. *The Road to Roses* is a beautiful reminder that even when you are shattered, the process of piecing yourself back together and becoming whole is not only divine but is the master plan.

KIMBERLY CALDWELL-HARVEY, TELEVISION HOST, SINGER

Desiree's honest voice and engaging story will captivate you with each turn of the page. With her desire to be true to who she is—who God made her to be—she navigated the spotlight. Through her story you will learn how to unpack the lies the world has told you so that you too can write your own fairy tale through the life you are living every single day. She invites you to live boldly, love hard, and follow the call that God has for your one beautiful life.

JENNA KUTCHER, HOST OF THE *GOAL DIGGER* PODCAST

Desiree Hartsock is an incredibly talented, passionate, kind, and honest woman. I admire her openness and vulnerability as she shares her heart with the world. Over the years, it has been an honor to watch her grow, fall in love, and build her happily ever after with Chris, Asher, and Zander. I am grateful to call Desiree one of my friends.

DEANNA STAGLIANO, STAR OF *THE BACHELORETTE*, SEASON 4

Desiree's story is a beautiful testament of God's grace and his ability to give us beauty for our ashes. *The Road to Roses* takes us on a journey of identity and ultimately reveals God's unending faithfulness in each and every season.

MARIELA ROSARIO, FOUNDER OF SHE SPEAKS FIRE MINISTRIES

THE ROAD TO
ROSES

THE ROAD TO
ROSES

Heartbreak, Hope, and Finding Strength
When Life Doesn't Go as Planned

DESIREE HARTSOCK SIEGFRIED

WITH AUTUMN KRAUSE

ZONDERVAN
BOOKS

ZONDERVAN BOOKS

The Road to Roses
Copyright © 2021 by Desiree Siegfried

Requests for information should be addressed to:
Zondervan, *3900 Sparks Dr. SE, Grand Rapids, Michigan 49546*

Zondervan titles may be purchased in bulk for educational, business, fundraising, or sales promotional use. For information, please email SpecialMarkets@Zondervan.com.

ISBN 978-0-310-36197-8 (audio)

Library of Congress Cataloging-in-Publication Data

Names: Hartsock, Desiree, author. | Krause, Autumn, author.
Title: The road to roses : heartbreak, hope, and finding strength when life doesn't go as planned / Desiree Hartsock Siegfried, with Autumn Krause.
Description: Grand Rapids : Zondervan, 2021. | Summary: "Desiree Hartsock was single, broke, and looking for love when she was offered the starring role on The Bachelorette, and she thought that she was getting everything she wanted. Now Desiree tells all in this honest reveal about the off-camera experience of the show, and her comeback journey to finding real love through it all"— Provided by publisher.
Identifiers: LCCN 2020058503 (print) | LCCN 2020058504 (ebook) | ISBN 9780310361947 (hardcover) | ISBN 9780310361961 (ebook)
Subjects: LCSH: Bachelorette (Television program) | Reality television programs. | Women on television. | Christian women—Biography.
Classification: LCC PN1992.77.B2454 H37 2021 (print) | LCC PN1992.77.B2454 (ebook) | DDC 791.45/72—dc23
LC record available at https://lccn.loc.gov/2020058503
LC ebook record available at https://lccn.loc.gov/2020058504

Published in association with the literary agency of WordServe Literary Group, Ltd., www.wordserveliterary.com.

Cover design: Curt Diepenhorst
Cover image: Brandon Hill Photos
Interior design: Phoebe Wetherbee

Printed in the United States of America

21 22 23 24 25 /LSC/ 10 9 8 7 6 5 4 3 2

To my husband, Chris.
God blessed the broken road that led me straight to you.
XO, Des

To my mom, Melanie.
Thank you for letting me write when I should've been doing
math schoolwork. You knew I was a writer before I did.
Love, Autumn

CONTENTS

PROLOGUE

It was supposed to be a fairy tale. Literally! My season as the ninth Bachelorette on ABC was branded as a modern-day fairy tale in which I was handed the keys to the castle. But in my case, they were the keys to a $224K turquoise Bentley and a Malibu villa complete with a mini design studio. I'm not complaining. Oh, and Prince Charming was part of the deal. Twenty-five Prince Charmings, to be exact.

I knew being America's Cinderella for three months would be akin to a glam yet grueling boot camp, but I was ready to find love. Prior to the show, I had begun to take my Christian faith more seriously. I knew who I was in Christ, and that identity was more important than any happily ever after that reality TV could offer. *Buuut*, I thought, *if reality TV can lead me to the man God has for me, then sign me up!*

. . .

Only, things took a turn. In fact, that's probably why you've picked up this book: to see what *really* happened with my very own He Who Must Not Be Named. Look, I get it. And you probably get it too. It's easy to allow ourselves to fall into old ways, old patterns, and old thoughts only to lose sight of who we are and what we want, to suddenly look around and think, "How did I get here?"

In my case, there was the added dynamic of four million viewers who watched our breakup on national television. Let me tell you: the aftermath wasn't pretty. The breakup trended on Twitter and was splashed across the covers of tabloids, which described me in extremely unflattering terms—namely, as the cover of *Us Weekly* put it, "humiliated, betrayed, and driven to tears."[1] Then when I accepted Chris's proposal, I was accused of being fake, and the internet at large declared that he was a "rebound."

Time has passed, and a marriage, a successful career as a wedding gown designer, and two beautiful children separate me from that chapter of my life. But here's the thing: that breakup has followed me. Just a few years ago, I was hooked up to a polygraph test by producers on a marriage therapy reality TV series so they could ask if I "settled" by choosing my husband.

So I want to tell my side of the story, once and for all. It's easy for people to define my season—even me—by that relationship, but that's not the whole story. He Who Must Not Be Named (okay, so his name is Brooks) wasn't the problem.

Even though I was dressed up in beautiful gowns that cost more than six months' wages at my old job, I was hiding deep hurts underneath my camera-ready smile. I knew God loved me and that I didn't have to do anything to deserve a happily ever after. But somewhere between the first night in the Bachelor mansion and the breakup in Antigua, I lost sight of those truths. That's the thing about old lies: they're hard to rewrite—and mine came back with a vengeance.

I needed to remember my identity in Christ and that it was *okay* to be me, wounds and all, even if I was ugly-crying in front of a whole camera crew in Antigua. Only after being "betrayed, and driven to tears" did I realize I'd forgotten the most important thing: I was already loved, and only because of that truth could I love someone else.

ONE

REJECTED!

"Rejected!"

—US WEEKLY

*This was the one-word headline slapped underneath
my photo after my breakup with Brooks. It was right
on the cover. Sometimes being a cover girl sucks!*

I sat on the dock. Stunned. The only sounds were the lapping of gentle waves against the dock and my sobs. I wiped tears from my cheeks and pushed windblown hair out of my face. Cameras circled around me, silent but present.

To explain how I got here, let's revisit the most embarrassing moment I've ever been blessed with (or more like plagued with) . . .

I thought it was just another day in the Bachelorette fairy tale and that I would be going on another date from the producers' playbook of epic dates. It would involve a sweeping view, some cool mode of transportation (horses, maybe, or more likely a helicopter), champagne toasts, and a perfect red rose waiting to be handed out or withheld.

The cast, crew, and I were in Antigua. I was down to my last three guys: Brooks, Chris, and Drew. I'd already had dates with the two other guys and was dying to see Brooks again. I hadn't seen him in the week since meeting his family, and while I still had questions for him, I wanted our date today to solidify our feelings. I hoped I would be pinning a rose boutonniere to his suit jacket that night. I worried, though, that something might go wrong.

Of the remaining guys, Brooks was the only one who hadn't expressed his love for me. "It's just the show," I thought. "He'll be more comfortable now that there aren't any other group dates and the end is in sight."

We'd been on several dates by this point, each one leaving me intrigued to find out more about Brooks. During the first date, I dressed up in a wedding gown and a veil, and he wore a tux. He picked me up, wedding gown and all, to lift me into the Bentley. It's safe to say he swept me off my feet, literally and metaphorically. My nerves, which had been jittery since the beginning of the show process, calmed at that moment because I knew I could relax in his arms . . . er, company. Afterward, we hiked to the Hollywood sign and sat on a grassy slope with the glittering panorama of Los Angeles spread out at our feet. I talked about how the sign reminded me of people chasing their dreams. Like many other starry-eyed idealists, I'd come to La-La Land to pursue some dreams of my own. Brooks confided in me about a past relationship. His face became pensive as he spoke about his last breakup, and it was apparent that the rejection had left a deep scar. But I could focus only on his fun-natured spirit and hope the past rejection wouldn't come between us.

A vivid sunset filled the sky, and I started the kiss count of the season right there below the Hollywood sign. Up until then, I intentionally hadn't kissed anyone. To this day, it still surprises me when the Bachelor and Bachelorette leads kiss the candidates on the first night. You've known them for only about five minutes! Maybe I'm more traditional than the other leads preceding me, but by the time I kissed Brooks, I not only knew his name (first and last!) but also, most importantly, that we had a connection we could build on.

Kiss completed and deemed very good by both parties, we went off to dinner. We were hand in hand and giddy with the childlike excitement you feel before Christmas morning because we didn't know what to expect next. We walked onto a bridge with a sparkling chandelier suspended over our table and a private concert playing just for us. Silly eighth-grade dance moves ensued, and those, combined with the sweet warmth from the bubbly, left me with a schoolgirl crush. I knew then that this date was setting high expectations for my other dates to come.

On paper, Brooks was everything I loved in a guy: sensitive, adventurous, creative—not to mention his shaggy-but-in-an-artsy-way hair. If only I could have read between the lines. As I mentioned, he was everything I was always drawn to. And that was the biggest problem of all.

. . .

Now, just a few short weeks from a possible proposal, I headed to my last date with Brooks (catamaran ride to Great Bird Island, followed by a candlelit dinner—don't mind if I do!). I waited by the blue-green water in a loose top mirroring the colors of the sea and with the ever-present mic tucked into the back.

Though I was excited for the date, I was exhausted, not only from the never-ending filming and relentless travel schedule but also from the emotional weight of the show. I'd been whittling my way down from twenty-five relationships to three, all while feeling horrible about sending really nice, genuine guys home. As the guys confessed their affection for me, fears I thought were buried came alive again. Because I'd lacked reciprocated validation for so long, its sudden appearance made me cling to what was safe.

My empathetic nature prevented me from focusing solely on my emotions, and I constantly considered the guys' feelings too. I'd been a contestant on the show before, and I knew what it was like to stand in an elimination ceremony, heart in your throat and your fate tied to a long-stem rose as cameras angle to capture the fear in your eyes. I thought being the one handing out roses would be easier. Though I was now an expert at pinning boutonnieres to lapels, I was overwhelmed, confused, and worn out.

Brooks made his way through a grove of trees, and I beamed, my heart leaping at the sight of him. I wanted to savor each moment together. But my excitement quickly faded when I saw the solemn expression on his face as he walked across the sand. Something wasn't right. As we reached each other, his body language was off and instead of holding me close, he quickly let me go after a half-hearted hug.

"What's wrong?"

"So hard . . ." he said. "Can we go over there?"

Immediately, my stomach plummeted, and we walked over to a bench out on the dock. My thoughts raced. I wondered if he was about to end our relationship, but I couldn't wrap my mind around that. We'd come so far and it'd been so hard. There was no way he could just throw that all away. Each step toward the bench felt like a step closer to doom.

We sat the way we always did: I draped my leg over his knee, and he held my hand. Slowly, he began.

"I just want to talk to you about how I feel. It's been hard. The whole thing."

"Talk to me," I said. *Talk to me.*

Those three words encapsulated a deep and old hurt: that I'd been searching for love for so long and no one could tell me the simple things I craved to hear. My family wasn't very open, even with each other. Feelings weren't expressed in words but in hard-to-decipher nods and one-liners. But I wasn't fluent in my family's particular language. I wanted to be told I was valued, and I carried that sentiment—*talk to me*—into every prior relationship with guys who couldn't express their affection for me, leaving me wounded and confused. My whole life, I silently begged for others to be open and honest with me, but I didn't know how to vocalize my needs either.

I'd given this hurt to God, but in the context of the show, it came back, and instead of turning to my identity in Christ, I fell into my old ways of seeking outside approval. I needed Brooks to affirm my value, and the more he withdrew, the more I wanted affirmation from him.

Brooks kept going.

"I really want to be madly in love with you, you know? This is even harder because you were so excited about us."

Cue ugly cry.

"Please. Don't cry. Why are you crying?"

I sobbed, pulled my knees up to my chest, and buried my face. Brooks kept talking. He said that he was sorry, that he wasn't feeling it, and that I was the best person he knew—but not for him. Blah, blah, blah. The same script from every breakup since the dawn of breakups.

When I spoke again, it was the old me talking—the one who'd been so hurt and lost and craving love. I said, "I don't know how it feels to have my feelings reciprocated. That's what really sucks. For once in my life, I was hopeful. I've never felt completely loved, and it sucks." Then I gave him the vulnerability I so deeply wanted but never got from him. I told him exactly how I felt. "I don't care that you just broke my heart. I love you."

Saying those words was hard. No one had ever given me the space to be vulnerable. But for once, I needed to be heard, so I made that space for myself.

Afterward, we walked back to the shore.

"I'm sorry," he kept repeating as we slowly headed down the path to the van that would take him away. Forever. "I'm sorry."

None of it made sense. I stared at him in disbelief and said, "I've done everything by myself, and that's why I was hoping to meet someone I could share my life with."

We lingered on the path, and he hugged me one last time. For a moment, I was stiff against his embrace, and then I wrapped my arms tightly around him as though I could hold on to what we had and undo everything that had just happened.

Then he walked off to the van, and that chapter closed. I

was surrounded by cameras and producers but so alone. I rushed back down the dock, sobbing and trying to shield my face with my hand as the crew chased after me. I was done, done with it all, and only wanted to be alone with my heartbreak.

But the show must go on.

I came into *The Bachelorette* confident. Despite being an introvert who never sought the limelight, I was flattered that I'd been offered the role and grateful for the rare opportunity. Before agreeing to be the lead, I devoted any spare time I had to praying for God's guidance on the decision and felt not only his peace but also confirmation that he'd opened these doors for me. Yet doubts crept into my mind, and they grew stronger as the show progressed. Did I deserve this attention? Did I deserve to find love at the end?

When I sat down on the dock, grief washed over me, followed by anger at myself. I'd fallen into my old ways, when I knew I deserved so much more. I'd been swept away by the handsome guy who gave me only crumbs of affection while I tried to maintain the relationship for both of us.

Staring into the green-blue water, I was crushed. I felt like Cinderella when she runs away from the ball at midnight and her gown turns back into sooty rags. My so-called Prince Charming had dumped me, and I was once again the hurting young girl from my past.

TWO

OLD LIES

The new star of ABC's *The Bachelorette,*
26-year-old Desiree Hartsock, didn't grow
up with a silver spoon in her mouth.

—*OK! HERE IS THE SITUATION*

Old lies—the ones we carry with us, the ones that tell us we aren't lovable, that we aren't good enough—can have many different origins. This is the origin of mine.

I sat in a closet, nine years old, hoping that the four thin walls around me would muffle my sobs. There, with the hems of coats and dresses brushing my shoulders, I poured out my hurt in gulping breaths.

Only here did I feel safe from the teasing of my older brother,

Nate, and the neighborhood kids. Or so I told myself. But I could still hear the hurtful words replay in my head. To my brother, they were just words that didn't carry any meaning, but for me, they were daggers that left deep wounds. Even though I was alone, they permeated the small, dark space, and worse, they pierced my heart.

While the words that layered on top of each other dug deep into my heart, my brother couldn't have known just how harmful they were for an impressionable young girl. For all I know, in his mind it was all fun and games. Unfortunately for me, those wounds became scars that shaped my identity.

When I was young, I never had an opinion. Nor did anyone affirm that my opinion mattered. Too often, my childhood script went like this:

> **Someone:** "What would you like to eat?"
> **Me, turning to my brother:** "I don't know, what are you having?"
> **Nate:** "I'll have a grilled cheese sandwich."
> **Me:** "Yes, I'll have the grilled cheese too."

Zoom in on Nate's eyes rolling and annoyance filling his face. Now as I watch my younger son copy and agitate my elder, I get to see a glimpse of what it may have been like for my brother growing up. Who wants a little sister being a copycat at any chance she could get?

To a fault, I wasn't particular about anything and just "went with the flow." This lack of decisiveness and confidence in my decisions, likes, and interests allowed outside influences to dictate my every move for years to come.

When I was growing up, "home" was a series of apartments, small houses, mobile homes, RVs, and even at one point, a tent. I spent a lot of my formative years watching the terrain whiz by from the back seat of my family's sedan as we zigzagged our way across the Midwest. Some of the time, Nate and I would get along and try to get semitruck drivers to honk at us. Other times we would fight ruthlessly over who got to lay their head where in the car. I typically lost the battle and would end up napping on the floor of the car, with the middle floor hump as a pillow.

My parents are hardworking, honest people. They gave me the greatest gift of all: they raised me to live in faith, the one thing that's always given me hope throughout life's ups and downs. Our itinerant lifestyle made me adaptable, open-minded, and always ready for an adventure. I get my work ethic from my dad and have memories of my mom dancing around the house worshipping and saying, "Today is a good day, a day for rejoicing, a day for God's power to work. Today I will love Jesus more than ever before."

Fancy cars and big houses never appealed to my parents, and not once did I hear them worry about their finances or complain about being overworked. They are the definition of living by faith and walking in love. Once, we moved from Indiana to Colorado with nothing more than a few bags because they felt the Lord was leading them there. My mom's wanderlust lives strong in me. Her ability to just up and leave without a care for possessions or relationships is as admirable as it is jarring. I've learned to enjoy the freedom of adventuring, but growing roots or getting attached to any house was impossible. I always found myself wondering, "Where do I belong?"

My parents worked hard to provide for us. Once we were old

enough, Nate and I were left to our own devices. Dinners were microwaved meals, and it was up to us to get ready for school in the morning and bed at night, as well as keep up with our homework.

With our parents busy working, Nate and I had ample time alone to get on each other's nerves. If you grew up with siblings, you understand. Most of the time, though, I was either too much or not enough. If I cried, my tears were ridiculed. I quickly learned to hide them behind a facade of indifference and a wall of defensiveness. But I wasn't only the victim. I became a fighter, quick to jab back—not verbally but with a toss of a pillow or a punch to the arm. Sometimes we would get into physical fights, which led to more crying and him getting in trouble. That punishment probably didn't help his opinion of me. Verbal praise and physical affection weren't in my mom and dad's parental repertoire. Because of that, the only things I heard about myself were from my peers and Nate, and they had plenty to say. I was an artistic and sensitive child who loved drawing (a passion that would lead me to pursue designing later in life), and the scrutiny chipped away at my self-worth until there wasn't much left. At this point, even constructive criticism hurt since I didn't have a strong foundation of confidence to stand on. The insecurities I began to have about my physical appearance were overwhelming as they paralleled the inner beliefs of myself.

The four walls of whichever closet space we had at the time became my refuge, and before long, I built walls around my heart as well, cemented in place by the words I heard and started to believe about myself.

"Be tough, don't cry," was my motto to overcome any emotion. I quickly adapted to get by, learning that if I enjoyed *Sesame*

Street or *Mister Rogers' Neighborhood* or anything similar, I would be labeled a "baby," a word that quickly became a trigger for me in any argument we had. Even though my feelings would get hurt, Nate was my older brother, and I longed for his affection. I became a tomboy in third grade because I wanted to prove myself to him and the neighborhood boys.

We lived in a double-wide manufactured home just north of Colorado Springs, Colorado, at the foothills, where wealthy neighborhoods were on one side of the highway, and our trailer park, apartment homes, and everyone else were on the other side of the highway. You could say it was on the "other side of the tracks" because, well, you also had to cross railroad tracks to get to our mobile home park. Often times while on the school bus a kid would scoff, "Why do we have to come to this side anyway?" as if "this side" was full of brigands and had no rule of law.

The kids in our neighborhood often played together in the street, and I always thought I could win Nate's approval by succeeding in whatever we were doing. I held my own against the guys in every single game we played, tackling them during football, blocking the basketball, and shimmying up any tree, pole, or obstacle faster than any of them. Proving my toughness became my mission. Any bumps or bruises would be worth it to garner Nate and the other guys' respect. To this day, I still have several scars on my knees from playing so rough.

In an effort to fit in with the boys and avoid teasing, I wore baggy pants and oversized T-shirts. I figured that if I looked like them, they would accept me. But there was no way that would happen. Nate let me play in the rough physical games, which often ended with me being beat up and bruised. But would he let me be an honorary member of the "boys" club? Absolutely not.

In hindsight, I know there was a lot going on under the surface with Nate, and with that I can empathize. Often his bedroom was a futon in our living room while I, as the girl, got the extra room. He may have struggled to make friends at school since we always moved at pivotal and formative ages for him. Adapting and socializing to meet new friends was a required skill, and his quiet nature around peers may not have helped. It also seemed like one thing after another was against him in his efforts to play baseball, a sport he excelled at but wasn't given the opportunity to play after a broken collarbone and missed tryout. I'm sure our nomadic lifestyle and the amount of independence we had as children made him as uncertain about the world as I was and that, in his own way, he longed for love and attention too. After all, it's hard to raise yourself.

One thing that made me feel secure as a child was praying. Every night, my dad prayed with me before bed, and I prayed for everything in my young life: my friends, my stuffies, to get good grades, for my teachers, and so on. Starting from the young age of six, whenever I went to the store, I prayed that I would find money, and more often than not, I would discover an errant penny or dime on the floor. Sometimes I even found a crinkled dollar bill hiding underneath a shelf. Keep in mind that this was back when coins and money were the main form of payment. Even when my prayer wasn't answered, I kept on praying each and every time. I wasn't asking for money because I wanted to be rich. Instead, I was seeking reassurance—reassurance that I was heard, that I wasn't alone, and that God desired to bless me. My young mind didn't have the comprehension to understand what I was doing, but I was practicing faith. I was praying for things and believing they would happen. Little Des had big dreams and wanted big things to happen in her life, even if she couldn't fathom the path to them.

I never did pray that my family's situation would change. Poverty had been the backdrop of my life for so long that it was like the air I breathed. It just *was* and I simply accepted it, and the difficulties that it brought, as normal. However, they were anything but normal.

Once, in first grade, my teacher talked to my mom because she'd noticed my hair was slick and oily. Little did she—or my mom—know I'd been adding bath oil to my bath every night, not knowing that it needed to be rinsed out if I got it in my hair. Another time in third grade, I threw up at breakfast. I should've been kept home, but even if my mom encouraged me to stay home, I wouldn't; I was tougher than a little vomit, I thought, and I loved school. So off I went, throwing up repeatedly before arriving on the bus and then some more once I got to school. I stayed in the nurse's room till school was over since my parents couldn't come get me, and a teacher had to drive me home.

Sometimes I didn't have the proper clothes to wear to class and was embarrassed to wear lounge shorts as daywear. Throughout fourth grade I had a super cute, second-hand, color-blocked pink coat. It was one of my only jackets and definitely my favorite. There were two rectangle-shaped pockets on either side of the zipper that were stitched onto the base of the jacket. Well, these pockets would not stay on! They continued to come loose from the jacket every time I wore it. I didn't want to have to ask my parents for another jacket, so as an independent and innovative little girl, I would take my mom's needle and thread and sew the pockets back on by myself. To keep from being embarrassed, there were a handful of times I would keep my hands in my pockets during recess at school to keep them from coming loose from the jacket and flapping down. This meant I would sit out of playing any game that involved using hands or would opt to stay inside to avoid the possibility of anyone seeing my faulty jacket.

Through everything, I was aware that I was different from the other kids who had parents to drop them off and pick them up and who came into each semester with brand-new outfits and shiny school supplies featuring characters from popular TV shows. I found compassion in the neighborhood kids who, in even worse situations, never judged.

In hindsight, it's interesting to see how I was plucked from obscurity to be placed in the spotlight to find my happily ever after, a "rags-to-riches" story. But the grim truth is that my life, from childhood to young adulthood, embodied the "rags" part of the phrase. I didn't sleep by a fireplace or have dirt on my face like Cinderella, but my childhood was defined by want, both emotional and physical. Those two shadows followed me for a long time.

When I was cast on *The Bachelor*, all of it came with me—the wounds and the walls and the wants. But God was working. And I don't mean only during my time on the shows and the opportunities that they ultimately gave me. I mean he was working in my heart way back in that small closet space. I now see that he heard my cries and had a plan for me, even though I wasn't aware of it at the time. At every step, he was drawing me to himself, whispering in the darkness to that young girl who longed for love and validation. He knew what I needed and that he was the only one who could give it to me.

It was impossible to see at the time, but God was taking the dark threads of my past and weaving them into a tapestry of redemption and beauty. I can see now that my transient child-hood made me open-minded, deeply appreciative of nature, and humble. I had an understanding that God is my ultimate home. My family's poverty taught me that happiness isn't found in huge shoe collections or luxury handbags, that real treasures are stored up in heaven, and to always give to those who are less fortunate. Even my brother's teasing is redeemed through God's love. Because of it, I'm stronger (both physically and emotion-ally), empathetic, and determined to stand up for those who've been hurt.

But while the truth that God was the only one who could perfectly love me awaited me, I didn't understand or live in the freedom of Christ for a very long time. No, it took a long jour-ney to truly set aside the lie that I was unworthy, a journey that involved the complete upheaval of my life on reality TV.

THREE

A CRUSHING CRUSH

From high school crushes (aka obsessions) to
short lived romances and butterflies to tears,
I've experienced all of the emotions a girl can
go through when it comes to dating.

—ME, IN A POST FROM MY BLOG TITLED "WHAT I
LEARNED ABOUT DATING AND FINDING 'THE ONE'"

The whispering voice of those old lies came with me as I transitioned from childhood to adolescence. Just as I fruitlessly sought validation from my brother, I began to seek it elsewhere. Of course, the results were the same.

Enter Luke (name changed to protect the innocent—or should I say, the guilty?), a dark blond–haired boy with piercing eyes and a stocky physique. I met him in sixth grade, after moving from Colorado Springs to Denver. From seventh grade to my senior year in high school, I pined over him, developing a schoolgirl crush that, well, ended up leaving me crushed.

For the first year, Luke didn't know who I was. I was trying to find my way in yet another new school. I was disoriented because I realized that the fashion currency from my old school—butterfly hair clips, baggy pants, and white eyeliner—had a negative exchange rate here. The student body paraded the halls in Gap tops and Lucky Brand jeans and smelled like an Abercrombie & Fitch store. I, on the other hand, had never set a foot inside any of those stores, and the term *prep* wasn't in my vocabulary.

However, I found my place somewhere unexpected: on the volleyball court. Volleyball quickly became both an outlet and a source of affirmation. I naturally took to the skills of bump, set, and spike. Although a volleyball can't talk, I developed a *Cast Away*–esque relationship with the ball. I felt as though that sphere of synthetic leather magically found its way to me. Over and over again, it glided through the air and fell into my view, where my waiting hands would propel it over the net with a strength I never knew I had. I loved crushing the ball over the net to the other side.

I'm not sure if it was because of my impressive skills or the spandex shorts we volleyball players wore, but whatever it was, some of the popular guys in school began to notice me. They didn't know my name, so I quickly became identified by my jersey number: 55. Older boys pursuing me made me retreat inward. Let's face it—attention and I go together like peanut butter and gummy bears. Let's just say, it isn't good. While the attention felt good at times, I wasn't used to it, and I certainly wasn't good at handling it. I might be able to hold my own in a game of football, but when it came to romance, I was about as natural as a fish out of water.

On top of that, my parents consistently petitioned for me not to date until I was sixteen. I, caught in my growing awareness of boys and the knowledge that every other girl in my class could date, bristled against the restriction. Though my parents didn't want me to date, they didn't go to great lengths to prevent it, so I was able to do what I wanted. I suppose that's one perk of having busy parents.

So when I saw Luke for the first time, I let myself fall. It happened in art class, and I was primed for a distraction. Usually, art class was a second home for me, but that wasn't the case at this school. The teacher was like Miss Hannigan from *Annie*. She didn't appear to like girls and showed little patience for our chatter. My elementary teachers had always encouraged my natural artistic abilities, but she didn't seem to care. Wounded, I never did return to an art class after that. But while the class didn't help my inner Renoir, it was the place where I first laid eyes on Luke.

The moment was straight out of a rom-com when the hot girl or guy walks into a room and instantly the camera focuses in slo-mo on their beautiful features, before panning out to the drooling onlookers.

I was that drooling onlooker as he entered the class to drop off a note for the teacher, and instantly, my heart leaped. Now, in rom-coms, this is when the onlooker, who is the most unlikely partner for the lead role, usually receives some smoldering eye contact and the flash of a smile to trigger the beginning of a Cinderella Hollywood story. I had no such luck. Luke barely glanced my way as he waved to his friends and fixed his gaze on another girl. I didn't mind being overlooked since we'd never once met face-to-face before, but that day was the beginning of the tumultuous journey of my first relationship.

In eighth grade, our overlapping friends and Luke's house being near our tiny apartment brought our worlds together. He was the quiet type, a middle son of three boys, and passive, but athletic with good looks. And honestly, what high school girl's criteria extends much beyond handsome? We would go months of seeing each other romantically and then months of not. During the off times, I would hang out with other guys or keep myself occupied with volleyball and partying. With my need for validation, I became quite the kissing bandit, but I never put any significance on those random pecks because nothing could fully distract me from craving Luke's attention. We would pass notes as we passed each other in the hallway. Many of my private missives ended up in another boy's hands, and I would be teased about them. I want to believe Luke never intentionally gave those up. Soon my thoughts were consumed by wanting full closure or full commitment.

I would never get either.

Then another toxic relationship developed—only I really didn't want to be part of it. It was with a girl who was first my friend, a girl I'll call Sabrina. As a friend, Sabrina was open and generous. We enjoyed chatting about boys, and she would often have friends over at her house to hang out. But there was another side to her. She could also be manipulative and conniving, in a charming way that drew everyone in. One day she wanted to drive her father's vintage Jaguar to the mall without asking. I was hesitant, but I followed her lead. On our way back from the mall, we heard a sputtering *putt, putt, putt.*

"Oh no!" she exclaimed, and we looked at each other in

disbelief as the Jaguar slowed to a stop and refused to start again no matter how many times Sabrina turned the key in the ignition. Panic filled me, but I tried to stay calm. As much partying and nonsense I was a part of during my high school years, it seemed like I had an angel watching over me, even when I wasn't living my best life. When the police would come to break up a party and hand out MIPs, I would have magically just walked out the back door a few minutes prior, oblivious that they were coming. When I could have been arrested as an accomplice to theft or for marijuana use, or gotten into trouble for other shenanigans, I somehow got a "get out of jail free" card each and every time. This protection left my record clean and my parents unaware.

Sabrina had to call her father to come start the car, so she was clearly in trouble. But I thought this was another incident to add to my list of lucky breaks, especially when I made it home without anyone in my family knowing. Or so I thought.

A knock came at our door. I opened it to discover Sabrina and her mother standing on our doorstep.

"Hello?" I asked, confused.

"I need to speak to your mother right now!" Sabrina's mother said, so angry she could barely speak.

"Okay . . ." Immediately, I knew something was amiss, but I yelled for my mom.

"Can I help you?" my mom asked, coming to stand behind me. The angry mother kept glaring at me while I desperately scanned Sabrina's face for answers.

"Our daughters took our Jaguar car to the mall without asking, and you need to do something about that. Your daughter needs to take responsibility for her actions and suffer the consequences," Sabrina's mom relayed to my stoic mom.

"Really? I didn't know this. Okay, thanks for letting me know," my mom replied graciously.

As the door closed, fire burned through my veins, flushing my cheeks red. "Did Sabrina tell on me?" I wondered. "I thought she was my friend!"

My mom never did punish me or ground me. If anything, she didn't like the way another mother told her what to do and left it at that. Not a peep more.

After this incident, my relationship with Sabrina changed drastically. Our friendship came to a grinding halt, and we became completely at odds with each other. Friends we had in common were told negative things about me from Sabrina that caused hurtful drama within our friend group. Eventually, even Luke became involved in the high school drama. Sabrina told Luke absurd gossip about me, which caused him to keep his distance for a while. Having gone through the training ground of my brother, I was tough and never let anyone know my pain or see me cry. I acted as though nothing happened, and life went on. I may have delivered a Best Actress–level performance with my nonchalance, but the walls around my heart grew even thicker, and the closet was once again my refuge.

At the end of senior year, the tension between Sabrina and me culminated in my getting suspended after she told the dean I'd been drinking during lunch. It was true, I had a sip at a friend's house, but I resented being told on. She also extended a couple of invitations to "take it outside" and hash it out in the field. I never did RSVP to those invitations because if there were a few things I'd learned from half falling asleep during church service, they were these: "A soft answer turns away wrath, but a harsh word stirs up anger" (Proverbs 15:1 ESV) and "a haughty spirit before a fall" (Proverbs 16:18). Also, she had no idea the strength I was packing after months spent training for volleyball, and I didn't want to hurt her, especially when I didn't even understand what she had against me.

During our senior year, Luke and I began sending each other sweet texts and talking on the phone every night. Luke played football. Even though I was working as a hostess at Outback Steakhouse and often busy leading my volleyball team to victory, I tried to make it to every one of his games.

By then our four-year-long rollercoaster relationship was still just "friends with benefits," and I'd had enough. I wanted to either be affirmed as an official couple or call it quits. I had tried to do this multiple times in the past, but this time I meant it.

After a football game one day, everyone headed to a local eatery, most likely Applebee's. It was tradition. The girls would flirtatiously eat fries and humor the football players as they bragged about their sacks and touchdowns. This time I sat in a booth and watched the other couples sucking face and the single girls and guys clamoring for one another's attention. I was over it. Luke's hand was on my leg, yet I wasn't his and he wasn't mine. I'd put so much energy into this "relationship" and turned down many other boys. It all felt like a waste.

The next day I called Luke. We chatted as we always did. I had a burning desire to tell him off for leading me on, but I couldn't do it. My strengths lie in note passing, not verbal communication. We said goodbye. *Click.* The call was over. Instantly, I knew I couldn't just let it go. I dug deep and called him right back.

Ring. Ring.

Luke answered.

"Hey!"

"Uhhh . . . ummm, hey. I know we just talked, but I really need to say something."

"Okay, what is it?"

"Well, you see . . . we have been back and forth and on and off for so many years." I paused. "And I've had it."

"Okay." Luke was thrown off.

I kept going.

"I no longer want to do this. If you want to pursue this as a relationship, then let me know—otherwise I am completely done. No more of this."

"Sure!" Luke said confidently.

Ummm . . . what? My thoughts came to a screeching halt.

"You want to be boyfriend and girlfriend?" I asked in disbelief.

Always a man of few words, he said, "Yes!"

"Okay!" I said. "Well, that's great then."

We chatted for a little while longer before we both said goodbye.

What just happened? My thoughts raced as a brick fell from the wall surrounding my heart.

Luke and I became inseparable. He was no longer unsure or unexpressive at school. He would hold my hand and kiss me whenever he saw me in the halls. Our relationship was different as night and day compared to what it was like before the call. Why? Was it the possibility of me walking away, or possibly that his brother moved away and he wasn't afraid of being teased about having a girlfriend? Or was it something entirely different? Maybe it was the seriousness in my voice and the conviction in my words. I stood up for myself for once and got what I wanted.

But not forever.

Just when things seemed perfect, old high school drama came roaring back.

After graduation I was determined to get out of Colorado as fast as my lipstick-red Pontiac Grand Am could go. Luke and I were very much in love, and I had no intention of breaking things off. We decided we would try a long-distance relationship as I headed off to California to attend fashion school and he played football in Nebraska. The plan worked well. I was fully consumed by my love for design and gave myself to my classes and learning. I had to work almost full-time to get by, so my partying days were gone for these few short years while I hunkered down to focus on my dream.

Since both of us were extremely passive, we always had pleasant visits and never any arguments or disagreements. We would simply enjoy each other's company. We had talked about marriage but never in the context of logistics or reality. A year into college, Luke went home for the holidays. My parents had already moved to Florida by this time, so I decided to stay in California and work instead. All our friends from high school got together at a party, including the notorious Sabrina. Since Luke and I had been together officially for about two years now, I never saw anyone as a threat, not even her. I never trusted the girl, but I did trust Luke and never thought he would hurt me. But a few days later, I got a call from a friend who was at the party.

"Hey, girl!" my friend said. "I need to tell you something."

My heart jumped straight into my throat. I'd spoken to Luke the night before, and he told me he and Sabrina had kissed at the party, but from the amount of concern in my friend's voice, it must have exceeded the little peck that he described.

I held it together to say thanks for the call and goodbye. Then

I dropped my phone to the ground. I bawled. My sobs encapsulated years of hurt, of not being good enough, of holding on to a hope that'd been destroyed in a single phone call. In the following weeks, I would find myself suddenly in tears during class, in the fitting room of my retail job as I cleaned up piles of clothes someone left behind, or as I stood under the rushing water of the shower. I couldn't go anywhere without the pain of betrayal following me.

Luke tried relentlessly to win me back after a watered-down confession. A steady stream of letters and flowers arrived at my doorstep to show how sorry he was. I didn't want bouquets or love letters. I wanted to trust again, to feel deeply loved again. He couldn't take my dismissals and asked if I would visit him in Nebraska. After months of reflecting, working hard, and studying, I decided to go. He had hurt me, but my loyalty and love for him wouldn't leave me.

I have a tendency to always think the best of others, which comes from DNA passed down from my parents. Despite his betrayal, I chose to see the good in Luke and to forgive him. That didn't mean I would forget his actions, but I couldn't allow anger in my heart to fester. I wasn't living the best life God wanted for me at that time, yet I still knew he was there and that he had good things in store for me. I have always held on to the notion that "the best is yet to come," which I believe allowed me to move on from the temporary heartache. Looking back, I see meaning in how the Lord restored my heart each time my brother or Luke wounded me. He didn't take away the pain, but I always had a sense that my future would be better and that I didn't need to be bitter. I also think that being hurt by my brother at such a young age and being unable to simply run away from him since we lived together taught me the ability to forgive much faster than I naturally might have. While I spent many days lost in a wave of hurt, ultimately I knew what I had to do to move forward and let hope guide me.

As hard as it was, I chose to forgive Luke.

And even harder, I chose to forgive Sabrina.

FOUR

TEXTBOOK TOXIC

Many of my significant memories of life, lessons and
growth come from [my time in Newport Beach].

—ME, IN A POST ON MY BLOG TITLED *"WHAT I LOVE
MOST ABOUT THE 11 CITIES I'VE LIVED IN"*

As I consider my life before *The Bachelor* shows and my life
now with my growing business, my marriage to Chris, and
our two beautiful boys, I am blown away. I see what I have and
am so grateful. But none of this would have been possible if I
hadn't changed directions and learned how to break old patterns
I had developed to protect myself—even though that process was
painful. I learned what it meant to break free of old patterns from
a relationship that could only be described as textbook toxic. The
relationship occurred when I was twenty-one years old. And it

paved the way for my missteps with other relationships down the road and, finally, with Brooks.

After my graduation from the Fashion Institute of Design and Merchandising in Los Angeles, I briefly moved back to Denver, where I'd lived for most of my high school years. I didn't stay long before breaking up with Luke and heading back to California with a one-way ticket to pursue my dreams of design. Though we'd stayed together after the Sabrina incident, I realized that the cracks in my heart hadn't healed. I felt terrible for hurting him after another year and a half as a couple, but as much as I loved him, something deeper had changed in me. I didn't belong in Denver, and I also knew in my heart that I didn't belong with Luke. I had grown and changed, and my priorities had too. I, for once, needed to do something for myself, rather than expend my energy on someone else's happiness. My passion for design and a life outside of Colorado was calling me. Though I'd sought Luke for many years, I was the one to leave of my own accord.

However, before I left for California again, I met someone in Denver.

I describe Denver as a small big city. It might not have the fame and celebrity of Los Angeles, but it has its own vibrant nightlife set against a backdrop of sloping, gray mountains.

I'd recently turned twenty-one, so I was able to get a job providing bottle service at a high-end martini club downtown. It was one of the fanciest places in the area, and I spent my shifts in a black dress, dark lipstick, and high heels, upselling expensive bottles of liquor to patrons with money to burn and discreetly googling how to pronounce fancy champagne labels behind the counter before heading out to serve. I was living a *2 Broke Girls* version of *Sex and the City*. Professional athletes and high-rolling businessmen came through the bar on a regular basis, and it was an exciting environment because you never knew who you might meet. Also, the tips didn't hurt!

One night, a handsome, vaguely familiar man was seated in my section. The slew of women (and men) staring at him and his group made me realize he was a professional athlete. I didn't have a lot of experience with guys (the only guy I'd dated at that point was Luke), but I was intrigued and struck up a conversation as I poured shots for him and his buddies. It turned out that he was quiet and had about as much personality as a sack of potatoes. However, I overlooked his faults because, well, he was handsome and sought after, and what girl in her early twenties isn't enamored of the idea of dating a professional athlete? Also, it was my first time dipping my toes into the pool of adult dating, so anyone who didn't have to borrow their mom's van to take me to the movies seemed sophisticated and mature.

Later that week, I was at a bar with some girlfriends when I saw "the athlete" across the way with a group of guys who also played on his team. I reapplied my lipstick, tousled my hair, and went in for the kill. Unfortunately, he hadn't developed any more personality in the few days since I'd last seen him, so while he was getting a drink, I struck up a conversation with one of his teammates, a guy I'll call Ryan. Ryan mentioned that he was from California, and I told him that I was moving back there in three weeks. Nothing else happened with Ryan aside from the simple conversation, but I was struck by his easy smile and that he was totally my type physically, with his dark hair and muscled physique (in addition to being able to maintain lighthearted talk, unlike his teammate counterpart).

Fast-forward and I'm back in California, full of optimism for the future—because I hadn't yet fallen into debt—and working at a plus-size clothing company and a sports bar in Newport Beach. The sports bar was much more casual than the martini club in Denver but boasted a retractable roof, which let patrons soak up glorious vitamin D and enjoy the salty tang of ocean air. The bar had an athletic theme, so the waitresses wore a sexy, decidedly inaccurate version of a lacrosse uniform: a short skirt, low-cut black top, and knee-high socks. I was working Fourth of July, and the weather was perfect, which meant the beach and every restaurant within a ten-mile radius of the shore was packed. I was heading to grab some beers for a group of customers when I turned around and ran smack-dab into Ryan.

"No way!" I exclaimed, projecting over the hubbub of the bustling bar. "Hey! Do you remember me from Denver?"

"Of course I do!" He flashed that friendly, easy smile of his. "What are the odds?"

I gave him my number, and we ended up hanging out that whole week. I knew he had to go back to Denver because his team was based there. Obviously, long-distance relationships aren't ideal, but I thought we could at least see where a relationship might go.

At the end of the week, we said goodbye and he headed back home. We talked on the phone, but he was distant. Something was off. I sensed he was pulling away, as though the miles between us were too many to overcome and what we'd shared in Newport Beach wasn't enough to carry us through. I wrote it off as him being busy, but a nagging intuition came over me, and I wondered if something else was going on.

A few hours later, I stalked him on MySpace (remember MySpace?). Finding his profile was easy enough, and I scrolled through his photo albums. Then I came across an image and froze. It was an instant stab to the gut and the fulfillment of the unsettled intuition I hadn't been able to shake. It was a photo of him with a girl, and it was recent. I dug further and puzzled, piece by piece, to find the truth. They looked like a couple. I don't think adequate words exist to describe what it is like to see that the guy you hooked up with a few days ago has a girlfriend—or what looks to be a serious relationship. Disbelief rushed over me, then confusion. I had given him so much of myself over that week, and he had selfishly taken it, not caring about me or his girlfriend.

This is where I wish I could say that I never talked to Ryan again because I knew he could never be a good boyfriend, much less a good husband. Loyalty and honesty are essential for any relationship, and Ryan didn't offer either. But when you crave love, you cling to any form of it, even if it's only a sliver of the real thing. To me back then, the sliver was better than nothing, and perhaps I believed it was all I'd ever get. Aside from not experiencing the kind of affection I longed for as a child, I spent years seeking reciprocated love from Luke. My lifelong rejections from those I wanted love from made me feel unlovable. That feeling got into my psyche at such a young age, and once entrenched, it took a lot of work, forgiveness, and the grace of God to eventually be free of it.

I knew I couldn't expect much from Ryan, but we kept in touch over the next few years. Every Fourth of July, he came out to Newport Beach and we would pick up right where we left off. Every time, it was like our first week together. Our chemistry was always electric, as though we hadn't been apart for the vast majority of the year.

Eventually, I had reasons to travel out to Denver. I didn't know if he had a girlfriend, and I couldn't bring myself to ask. I lived on the displays of affection he offered me while we were together, never demanding more because I told myself they were enough.

One time, after a few years, we met up at a bar in Denver, and it was only the two of us. It felt like we could shut out the world and truly see each other. We talked about our lives and shared our hearts, and I wondered if this could be the start of something more. He took me back to where I was staying, kissed me, and left.

It was several days before he texted again.

That's how our relationship went. It was a game of cat and mouse, and it kept going on and on. Ryan would give me attention, then it would abruptly stop and I wouldn't hear from him for a long time. I was always unsure of where I stood with him or whether we would ever meet again. Through it all, I accepted it and made excuses for his behavior.

Eventually, I started a relationship with another guy, who I will call Andrew. I'll share more about him later. Suffice to say, though he was more committed to me than other guys had been, the dysfunction I'd come to accept with Luke and Ryan was now an established pattern for this new relationship.

Fourth of July came around again, and Andrew and I were on a break. I wasn't fully seeking God yet, but I was on the verge of pursuing my faith more seriously, and I was starting to have doubts about Andrew. With booze, lots of poor decision-making, and fireworks over the ocean, Ryan and I met up again.

Many women can relate to having a guy come in and out of our lives, stringing us along by lavishing attention on us and then taking it away. It's awful and toxic and leaves us in a horrible limbo between hope and hurt. Even if the right guy comes along, we've become used to and been so damaged by the confusion that we can't see the good in someone else. Ryan had gotten under my skin so much that even after I eventually ended things with Andrew and started to grow as a Christian, I had a moment of weakness and reached out to Ryan. Why is it we always want what we feel we can't have?

He'd been released from his team recently and was living in Venice, California, close to Newport Beach. We hung out a few times, but our ugly pattern immediately reemerged, the one where he would give me attention and then go radio silent. I was left, once again, in the horrible place of wanting to text and call him—wanting him to talk to me—but knowing, deep down, he would never offer anything more than a casual hookup. I kept my mind and calendar busy pursuing other guys to try to keep myself from pondering the "what ifs" with Ryan.

Finally, I was done. I'd been seeking God and could tell that this relationship was distracting me from finding real love. Real love is sacrificial, a giving of oneself to another, a commitment that places the needs of the other person before our own. The relationship with Ryan was the opposite. It wasn't giving; it was vampiric. And it'd gone on for so long that a lot of life and hope had been drained out of me.

Right before I moved from Newport Beach to Los Angeles, Ryan and I cut all ties. As freeing as it was, the patterns from that "relationship" were deeply ingrained in me. A friend, knowing I needed a fresh start, convinced me to go on Match.com and accept a date with a cute guy who'd moved to Los Angeles by way of Ohio. I'll call him Liam. He had none of the artistic moodiness and commitment phobias I often found in LA guys. Instead, he was like a handsome, young Mister Rogers—respectful, really sweet, and able to express his feelings. He even worked with special needs kids. I mean, I don't think he could have been any more wholesome and ideal.

"How did it go?" my friend asked me as I kicked off my heels in the living room, having just gotten back from the date.

"He's really . . . nice," I said, thinking hard. "I'm just not sure if it's there."

Liam made attempts to pursue me, and after months of dating, I realized he was the perfect kind of guy for me—thoughtful, mature, expressive, and ready to settle down. But regardless of his charm, I had the inexplicable urge to end things. When I saw how straightforward and honest he was, it made me antsy, and everything in me wanted to flee. So I ended it. My emotions infuriated me. Why couldn't I be with him? He was basically the antonym of Ryan.

In truth, the stability and health Liam represented terrified me. I was at the beginning of growing in my faith and had yet to embrace my identity in Christ. Dysfunction felt safer to me. It was horrible, but it was familiar and confirmed my distorted view of myself.

What's funny is that Chris, my husband, and Liam are so similar. They are both thoughtful, steadfast, and charismatic, bringing joy to everyone around them. Thankfully, I was very different when I met Chris. By then I'd spent the past year fully seeking God and set aside time every day to pray and read my Bible. I'd given up my life of hard partying and my relationship with Andrew. Through the grace of God, I slowly released the lies about myself that I'd carried for so long and found victory in his truth. Because of that, I was able to enter the first healthy relationship of my life with Chris (of course, this was severely complicated when I fell back into old patterns with Brooks—stay tuned for that).

I had one final moment with Ryan after filming *The Bachelor*—I received a text from him.

"Leave me alone," was my first visceral thought. Slowly, I read the text. I was still reeling from the show and eager to get back to work, but Ryan made his way to the front of my thoughts. I thought about seeing him again, but I knew I had already moved on. Of course, I didn't delete the text thread.

Ironically enough, right before I was chosen to be on *The Bachelorette*, Ryan sent me the kind of invitation I had always wanted from him. He'd been invited to a wedding that summer and was wondering if I would be his date. This was different from a casual hookup. A wedding was a formal event, and I'd meet his family and friends. My mind got carried away, and emotions I thought I'd dealt with came back. Maybe this was everything I'd always wanted. The part of me that had longed for him for so long said, *"Finally!"*

But the other part of me was stronger. That part stood in defiance. Slowly, deliberately, I texted him back: "Sorry, I'm not available."

I didn't know what the future held. I knew I was in the running for *The Bachelorette*, and my financial life was more precarious than ever before. I did know one thing, though. I knew God had already done a great work in me and that I no longer wanted to feel like I wasn't enough. I knew I wanted more for myself and more stability in a future partner. From there on out, I knew I was treasured and beloved and that anyone who couldn't treat me like I was didn't deserve my hand . . . much less my heart.

FIVE

ROCK BOTTOM AND BIG RISKS

[Desiree] now chooses faith over everything.

—*MINT ARROW MESSAGES PODCAST*

With a thankful heart, I can say it's true.
But it wasn't always that way.

When I applied for *The Bachelor*, I had just recommitted my life to the Lord, even though that meant ending things with Andrew, someone I loved very much.

Andrew was cut from the same fabric as Luke, Ryan, and my family—quiet and inexpressive of emotions. He was exactly what

I was used to, and the empath in me, which is always drawn to those I think I can help, was immediately intrigued.

Our relationship was the perfect example of how childhood wounds follow us into adulthood and create dysfunctional patterns that are nearly impossible to break. As painful as it ended up being, dating Andrew taught me invaluable lessons about myself.

So how did I meet him? Here goes.

• • •

After I graduated from the Fashion Institute of Design and Merchandising, I settled in Newport Beach, which is a dream of a coastal city in California. There, I dove into the deep end of the party scene. Life was a lot easier when buzzed. Hurts from my past and stress from my empty bank account couldn't touch me once my blood alcohol level was elevated.

As I mentioned, I worked as a waitress at a sports bar right on the shore and clocked out every evening with salt from the ocean breeze in my hair and the warmth of the sun on my skin. My lifetime love affair with the beach began there—to this day, I swear that I have sunshine and saltwater in my veins. The weeknights were devoted to partying, and the weekends were extensions of the nights: full days spent in a wash of sun, sand, and sangria. I was young, as was my liver, and we both worked overtime.

At the same time, I dreamed about becoming a wedding gown designer. I had a degree from FIDM and had worked at a variety of bridal salons where rows upon rows of exquisite gowns hung from gold racks. I was swept away by their beauty and how they transformed a woman into a bride. Words like *tulle*, *ball gown*, and *lace* became my love language, and I wanted nothing more than to design wedding gowns myself. During my thirty-minute lunches, I poured over wedding magazines and designers' lookbooks in the breakroom, studying the different styles. But the harsh truth was that I had zero connections, zero portfolio, and zero money. Still, I was determined to make my dream a reality, and I got a job at a plus-size women's apparel company to gain hands-on experience. However, California sunshine comes with a heart attack–inducing price tag. It turns out happy hour margaritas and bottom-shelf bourbon can make you feel good, but they can't do much about postcollege poverty.

Most of my friends were bankrolled by parents and had family as their financial safety net. I, however, was alone on the tightrope of young adulthood, with nothing and no one to catch me if I fell. And fall I did as setback after setback plagued me. I got into multiple car accidents. My roommate's dog peed on our carpet and we lost the security deposit. I basically lived in indentured servitude, but no matter what I did, I couldn't make ends meet and slipped further and further into debt. My finances were a comedy of errors I couldn't escape, even though I was juggling my day job and waitressing evenings and weekends. That's when I met Andrew.

We met on a sunshiny day, the idyllic sort that you see on sitcoms set in Santa Monica or Venice. The beach was full of sun worshippers lying out on towels, workout nuts jogging up and down the shore, and yuppies walking their tiny, well-accessorized dogs. I was at a friend's housewarming party near the beach. The plan was to see the new place, do some pregaming, and then head to the bars on the peninsula. I wasted no time downing an array of Jell-O shots mixed with some stiff concoctions, and they did their thing. Oh, hello buzz.

Somehow I didn't hear the calls for everyone to meet up outside and head off for the bars, and before I knew it, I was alone in a huge house full of half-empty beer bottles and discarded red plastic cups.

"Hello?" I called out, but the only response was my voice echoing off the ceiling. In my less-than-clear-headed state, searching the house for anyone else who'd been left behind seemed like a good idea. Holding on to the bannister for steadiness, I made my way upstairs. The first bedroom was empty. The second one was empty as well. So I tried the third one, stumbling into it like a drunken Goldilocks.

A guy was there, and he seemed to be in worse shape than I was. He was passed out on the bed, but that couldn't hide the fact that he was one of the most handsome guys I'd ever seen. I'm talking brown hair and Apollo-like features—the whole nine yards of handsome. I shook him, and he groggily opened his eyes.

"Who are you?" I asked, as though he was an intruder in my home instead of vice versa. My question didn't seem to deter him. Instead, an amused smile crossed his lips.

"I'm Andrew."

A few hours later, we'd caught up with our friends and stood together at a bar on the Strand. Off in the darkness, waves lapped the sand, and lights from distant boats dotted the horizon. We were beyond flirtatious with each other, and in a moment when we weren't chasing down shots, we found ourselves staring into each other's eyes and stumbled into our first kiss—fireworks. That was all it took. We fell for each other. Hard. Or maybe only I did.

Soon we were spending every moment together. No matter what we were doing, from sunbathing on the sand to biking side by side down the Strand, we would end up in a breathless tangle of limbs and passionate kisses.

After a while, though, our connection couldn't mask deeper problems. Undeniably, our chemistry was the real-life equivalent to the fire emoji, but a relationship built on attraction is doomed to flame out. Andrew was emotionally unavailable and closed off. It was clear that we loved each other, and our relationship had all the trappings of commitment. Yet for a long time, the only thing he could say was, "I like you a lot."

Case in point: about five to six months in, Andrew and I were cuddling on the couch and watching a movie, which was our thing when we weren't out partying.

The romance in the movie heated up, and concurrently, so did my thoughts. "I really love this guy," I realized. Andrew leaned over and whispered, "I really like you."

I couldn't contain myself, and before I knew what was coming out of my mouth, I said three little words that my heart desperately wanted to hear back. Keep in mind that they were three little words that I'd kept locked away because I didn't want to use them loosely and I wanted to safeguard my heart from ever getting hurt again. But it's funny how feelings tend to have a timeline all their own and bubble up when you least expect them.

"Well, I love you," I hopefully stuttered.

A few seconds went by.

Nothing.

My heart raced. I was furious with myself. *Des! Why did you go and do that? You know you wanted him to say it first.*

We both turned our attention back to the screen, but my

heart fell like a bag of bricks. I was thankful he couldn't see the embarrassment on my face. It took probably another two months before he returned those words to me.

No girl wants to feel that they love someone who doesn't love them back—but love is funny like that and makes you believe something is worth fighting for even when it isn't right.

I justified his behavior because it was all I knew. Everyone, from my family to other boyfriends, struggled to share verbal affirmation. As an impressionable child, the lack of affirmation hurt and made me withdraw. As an adult woman, it made me accept far less than I deserved from the men—boys, really—that I dated.

I'm not exactly sure what made me realize that I needed so much more. I had tried everything else to cover up the deep pain in my soul, only to discover that once my buzz faded or Andrew wasn't there to distract me, it was just me, alone in my hurt. I think my realization that I needed more was a quiet awakening, growing from a seed of faith that had lain dormant for a long time.

Gradually, over several months, I grasped that my lifestyle of nonstop partying and even my relationship with Andrew were only temporary fixes that left me even more anxious and unsettled than before. I began to pray, attend church, and read my Bible more. As I did, I was slowly set free from a lifetime of hurts and lies. What's more, as God reconciled my heart to his, he also began healing the broken bond between me and my brother. My brother would send prophetic words to me through texts during this time that reassured me of our spiritual sibling connection as well as the Lord's will in my life. Just as I was questioning leaving my design job, he texted a word pertaining to

God's provision in my life. Just as I was questioning my relationship with Andrew and seeking clarity, my brother texted a verse
of strength to help me through. He was actively praying for me
and following the Lord's promptings, without ever knowing what
was going on in my life.

. . .

As I sought to learn God's will for me, I was particularly drawn to
the Gospels. I read the parable where Jesus speaks about pruning
a vine so that it will grow new fruit and was encouraged that God
was ridding me of my sins, my poor choices, and my unhealthy
pattern with relationships so that I would be renewed and able
to grow new fruit in my life.

Although I grew up with Scripture and faith, there is something so pure when you seek after it yourself. Truths reveal
themselves to you, and a passion to share God's love with others
rises up inside you. I had always known the story of God creating
the world, but only now when I read it for myself did I realize it
meant I was made for a purpose. In the story of Jesus dying for
my sins, I slowly allowed the truth that I was worthy of love to fill
my heart. In the story of the Holy Spirit being sent to believers
as a comfort and a helper, I no longer felt alone.

These truths made me blossom in ways I never had before.
The more I embraced them, the more distant I became from
Andrew and the more dissatisfied I became with hard partying. I
knew I should end things with Andrew, but he expressed interest
in going to church with me. Soon, though, our toxic dynamic
reappeared in this new area of life. Just as I did the work emotionally in our relationship, I began to do it spiritually as well. I

fought for his faith, not understanding that belief is a personal thing that no one can have for you. I realized this when we went to his sister's wedding in Chicago.

The pastor referenced various Bible verses, encouraging the couple to have a Christ-centered marriage. The bride mentioned how the groom was her best friend, her rock, and the one she could turn to at all times. In return, the groom said his own loving sentiments.

As I sat in the church, holding Andrew's hand and listening to the vows, warm tears formed in the corners of my eyes, but not because of the beautiful moment for the couple, as lovely as it was. Rather, I realized I wanted everything they had—and that I would never have that with Andrew. Try as I might, I couldn't envision us one day standing at the altar and exchanging such heartfelt vows. Sitting there, I remembered a piece of relationship advice that my dad had always told me growing up. It was inspired by 2 Corinthians 6:14. He said, "Make sure to be equally yoked!" When I first heard this, all I could think about was hardboiled eggs, but now I understood. It was important to have a lifelong partnership with a person who shared my beliefs. I had to learn this the hard way. Just because someone says they're a Christian doesn't mean you are instantly "equally yoked." You must test the waters of faith with a potential partner to gauge the sincerity and strength of their faith. This became apparent with Andrew and me.

Eventually, I knew I couldn't ignore the hard facts. Faith had become so important to me that I knew I needed it in a relationship, even though I'd never experienced it firsthand.

Ending that relationship was deserving of all capitals: *HARD*. Think crying in bed with dirty hair and two-day old pajamas. It also took several tries. Yes, we did the on-again/off-again, are-they/aren't-they thing because when you love someone, breaking up is awful, even if you know the relationship isn't right. We were living together, so we had the added difficulties of a combined lease and dividing up custody of the furniture we snagged off Craigslist. We also shared bills, so on top of being heartbroken, the breakup put me right back into the financial hole that had consumed me before.

I think what was really sad is that we cared deeply about each other. However, I was moving forward and saw he had issues I couldn't fix and that I had issues of my own to work on. Breaking up with Andrew was a huge step for me and one that demanded a lot of sacrifice. I moved into a friend's house and took inventory of my life, and let's just say it wasn't pretty. Andrew was gone. I wanted to be a designer but had no portfolio and not even enough money for a computer equipped for drafting. With no one else to rely on, I worked as much as possible and came home bone tired every single night. I knew I'd done the right thing, but that didn't make it easy. Sometimes doing the right thing just sucks, and we're left wondering if it was worth it.

I was at rock bottom with no hope of things getting better, much less pursuing my design dreams.

But, looking back, I think those desperate circumstances were a key step in my growth. I was forced to believe God would take care of me, and it's in those situations, when things are their scariest, that you can trust God and take big risks. That was the case for me. Also, without the distraction of a relationship or the desire to jump back into one, I had more time to focus on what was important. I took intentional walks to spend time with the Lord and wrote poetry as an outlet for healing and gratitude.

Many times while walking I would come across a rock, a grass patch, or cloud in the sky, all in the shape of a heart. And each time I felt as though it was a little wink from God affirming his love for me. One special day I was having a tough time, and while on my walk I asked God to speak to me. Within a split second a deer came down the hill, crossing the path behind me, and I began to weep. I had never seen or heard deer to be in this area of Los Angeles, but even without this knowledge, I knew it was the Lord's doing. With each new day, I was being renewed and restored in my faith, and as I grew in that area, I began to feel ready for the next chapter God had for me.

It was then that I walked into my apartment to find my roommate watching a little show you may have heard of: *The Bachelorette*. I had never seen an entire episode before, but I watched a bit over her shoulder. Something about the beautiful Bachelorette garnering the respect and affection of multiple men spoke to me. On top of that, I noticed that the cast traveled a lot, and the different international destinations were a siren call to my wanderlust heart.

A few nights later, while sitting on my bed in the bluish glow of my barely working, secondhand laptop, I saw an ad to apply to be a contestant on *The Bachelor*. That application, which seemed so inconsequential, would change everything.

SIX

NO HOME FOR THE HOMETOWN DATE

"The Most Uncomfortable Hometown
Dates in *Bachelor* History"

—*A HEADLINE FROM PEOPLE*

Guess whose hometown date is #2 on People's list?

I'm sure you are wondering how I ended up on two seasons of a show watched by millions when I had such humble beginnings. Fast-forward: I was twenty-five, completely broke, newly single, and living (a.k.a. barely surviving) in Southern California. I wanted to pursue my dreams of becoming a designer, but in actuality, I exhausted myself with nonstop work at a bridal salon.

It was then that I filled out the application to be on *The Bachelor*. Funnily enough, though I knew the premise of the show, I'd never watched a full season and had no concept of how popular the show is. But I'd been taking my faith seriously and thought that if being on the show was God's plan, he could open the right doors and maybe I could meet the love of my life. And even if the show didn't bring me "the one," there was the travel. Who doesn't want a free vacation staying in fancy hotels? Since I had seemingly endless work weeks and mounting credit card debt, the show sounded like a refreshing break from reality. I also dreamed of becoming a wedding gown designer but, in my current struggle to survive, had no time for sketching. *Maybe*, I thought, *I could do that between filming and possibly even make some plans for building a design business when I have free time*. I clicked *Apply*.

The application asked, "Why do you want to find love on TV?"

I typed, "Because it's not happening in Los Angeles, so why not?"

My response was both casual and honest and epitomized how I approached the entire casting process. It's also the reason I was ultimately selected. I knew everything was in God's hands, so I was simply myself at each step. Later, the producers told my parents that's what made me stand out—I was straightforward and heartfelt, without any need just to be on TV or desire to promote myself. I appreciated the acknowledgment since so many viewers assume that *The Bachelor* and *Bachelorette* cast are fame seekers who only care about building their Instagram accounts.

After clicking *Submit* on the application, I went to bed and got up early for work the next day without giving it another thought.

Never in a million years did I think anything would come of it. But, to my surprise, a few days later the casting department called, asking if I would come to an on-camera audition. Believe it or not, I was so busy that I didn't end up scheduling the audition, and then when they asked if I could go to a group casting event at a city I would be visiting, I missed that one as well. I can only say that my being on the show was God's will, because how else can I explain their persistent interest when I was essentially MIA?

After playing phone tag for a few weeks, I was invited to partake in a group casting call they were having in Los Angeles. For most contestants, it was probably an anxious yet exciting opportunity. Don't get me wrong, I was excited, but also I had been working my tail off day in and day out for the past year, and a required one full day of casting was more like a God-sent holiday for me! Also, I didn't care how the verdict read in the end. I would be myself and if that was enough, then so be it.

At work later that week, I headed to my lunch break. Every shift, I had only about thirty minutes to rest my aching feet and take a bite of a granola bar before heading back to tend to brides and straighten the racks of wedding gowns. I picked up my phone and saw I had a voice mail. It was the head casting producer requesting that I call her. Immediately, I returned the call. The producer answered and said, "Desiree, we would love to have you on the next season of *The Bachelor*!"

My reaction: complete shock. A few seconds passed as I gathered myself.

"Really?" I asked, dumbfounded.

"Yes!" She exclaimed.

Never in a million years was television, especially reality TV, something I wanted to do. I've always been a private and guarded person.

Me? On TV?

It was honestly laughable.

But I had been putting my trust in God, and I thought, "Maybe God sees something in me that I have yet to see in myself."

"Okay," I responded.

I'm not an overly effusive person. It's probably because of my years of wanting to conform and being raised by my taciturn parents. Whatever the case, my internal hard drive is wired to bury any excitement I feel. But when I got off the phone, my spirits lifted, and I couldn't stop the huge grin that spread across my face. I thought, "Finally, a chance for something new."

A few days later I received the contract, and with no experience and no one to help advise me, I signed it. Then I told my parents. I wasn't sure how they'd react because they are conservative, and I thought they might balk at the idea of their daughter dating a man who was also pursuing twenty-five other women— all while being filmed. At different times, I myself was conflicted about whether it was appropriate to participate in what would essentially be an open relationship. But my parents' response was surprisingly positive, and that, along with lots of prayer, gave me the peace I needed to continue.

Taking a deep breath, I packed my entire wardrobe, which consisted of a few dresses that verged more into the sundress territory than sophisticated cocktail attire and lots of black, retail-appropriate work slacks from the sale section of Ross Dress for Less and Marshalls (yes, I was so poor that I needed discounts on top of the already marked-down prices). I couldn't afford an evening dress for the first night, so I created one of my favorite red dresses of all time. I spent the last two weeks prior to the show working long days at the bridal salon and then coming home to sew my dress. I was like Cinderella getting ready to go to the ball—only without any seamstress mice and bird friends to help. I'm still shocked I finished the dress on time.

According to the instructions we received, we were allowed to bring up to three bags, but everything I owned fit into a single large duffel. Nothing is provided to the contestants on the show, so I also had to brush up on my makeup collection. As a bona fide beach girl, I wasn't accustomed to wearing anything more than mascara and eyeliner, but I knew a girl needed so much more for TV. With about twenty dollars and several YouTube tutorials, I figured out which drugstore makeup would be best for on-screen and how to apply it.

Two days before the first night of filming, a car was sent, and I was whisked away to a hotel where the cast was sequestered apart from each other. I was getting over a cold, so I continually sipped hot toddies to ease my sore throat before the big day. The last thing I wanted was to sound like a chain smoker for my national television debut!

The big night came, and I slipped into my red dress and went downstairs to the hotel lobby. I and the other contestants would be loaded into limos in groups of five to meet the Bachelor, Sean Lowe, and would attempt to charm him with our witty (cheesy) pickup lines. I stood there in my handmade dress with my bangs swept to the side because that was a thing that year and met the other contestants. For a moment, I felt like I was at a Miss America pageant. The other women were dressed in sparkly designer gowns, flashed smiles to reveal professionally whitened teeth, and wore enough brand-name perfume to threaten the air quality of anyone within a twenty-foot radius. The scene was almost a replay of when I was a child at school and saw the other kids with their trendy new clothes. Regardless, I was hopeful and determined to do nothing more than be myself. I'd learned the day prior that Sean was the Bachelor, and I knew he was a devout Christian, which was something I wanted in a partner.

Before I knew it, we'd boarded our limo and made the drive from the bright nighttime lights of Los Angeles to the dense, woodsy darkness of Malibu. I held my breath as the limo slowed to pass through a set of fancy gates and inched its way across the iconic Bachelor mansion courtyard. It came to a final stop across from Sean. It was go time. I got out of the limo, mentally repeating my directions—stand still for a few moments outside the limo (hi, America), cross to Sean (don't trip), introduce myself (also, don't forget my own name).

That first night, the contestants broke out a number of tactics to capture Sean's attention. One girl even wore a wedding dress and veil (I should've helped style her!). I kept my introduction simple. I'd brought two pennies, and we tossed them into the stone fountain that sits right in front of the mansion to make a wish. It's funny that I chose pennies. I didn't realize the irony at the time. If you recall, I used to pray to find money in the grocery store, and whenever I saw a bright bit of glinting copper, it was like a hug from heaven—a reassurance that I was heard and loved.

As I tossed my penny into the Bachelor mansion fountain, I wished for God's will to be done and that Sean could be the sort of partner who would love me and hear me.

However, things quickly became complicated. My walls were up as I struggled to protect my heart and discern my thoughts. Initially, Sean and I had natural chemistry and easy conversation, but they were the sort that good friendships are based on. Honestly, Sean wasn't "my type." But since he was the first guy I'd ever dated who was a man of God, I wanted our relationship to work. We aligned on our faith, and, I rationalized, that was the most important thing, even if our compatibility was as flammable as a wet birthday candle.

Many times I questioned whether I should stay on the show. At one point in Montana, when the drama was reaching its peak, with Tierra (the villain of the season) presiding at its apex, I began to doubt everything. I couldn't tell how Sean felt about me, and his decisions made me wonder if I wanted to be with him. I contemplated for a while, taking time to sketch out the beautiful Montana scenery from our perched porch, write in my journal, and turn to Scripture. Ultimately, I decided to stay.

We all know my stay was short-lived, and it became clear on my hometown date that Sean and I were not meant to be, which in and of itself was depressing. The other contestants had their hometown dates in the states and homes they grew up in, but it wasn't so simple for me. I'd lived in many different places, and none of them had a sense of "home" for me since my parents had long since left them. To make it work, my parents and brother came out to Los Angeles to film the hometown date at the house I was currently renting. I'd hardly seen my parents or Nate over the past eight years because they'd moved to Florida and then Ohio, and none of us could afford to visit one another. Leading up to the date, I heard the other girls talking about their seemingly perfect and happy family lives, and insecurities overcame me. Would Sean be able to accept who I was? And what would the dynamic be like when I finally saw my family for the first time in so long?

The daytime portion of the date, which was just Sean and me, was a hike on a trail, and I went into it unsure. Mine was the fourth hometown date, and Sean had been traveling and processing a lot. As we first ran to each other to get our date started, I could tell he was tired and withdrawn, but I tried to keep my perkiness and positivity alive. We walked up to an observatory area that overlooks Los Angeles, and I shared with him a poem I'd written. It was the one way I felt I could tell him I was falling for him without saying I loved him. Because truth be told, I wasn't in love at that point in our relationship, but I knew I needed to share something with him. He seemed to like it, but even our body language felt off. This made me even more anxious for the night portion of the date. A prank was planned to get Sean back for the prank he did to me on our first date. This involved a fake ex-boyfriend knocking on the door to win me back during our date. With the daytime portion being good but not great, I was unsure how Sean would take it.

The evening was as awful as I feared. Sean did not enjoy or find humor in the ex-boyfriend prank, and I could tell he was more annoyed than anything.

My family arrived, and I went off to chat with my parents while Sean talked to Nate. I tried to express how I felt about Sean to my parents, but they were even more quiet than normal, thrown off by the cameras circling us. We rejoined Sean and Nate in the living room, and immediately I knew something was very wrong. Sean was pissed. Really pissed. I could see it in his eyes, which flashed a thunderous blue. He struggled to contain himself and was gracious to my parents, but he couldn't wait to get out of there. Confused and scared about what Nate had told him, I said goodbye to Sean outside and went back in.

"What did you say?" I asked Nate. "What did you say to him?"

"I told him he's a playboy," he responded. "This whole show is a joke. It won't work out for you."

I really wanted Nate's approval, but instead I just felt more confused by his words. The walls I'd so painstakingly erected around my heart weren't enough to protect me. Once my family left, I cried for the first time that entire season.

I went into the rose ceremony completely drained. Before Sean started handing out roses, I asked to talk to him. Part of me already knew our relationship was over and that this conversation was a Hail Mary. Still, I wanted him to understand. Maybe my brother was abrasive and I wasn't exactly Martha Stewart, but I wanted to fight for us—and for him to fight for me, when no one else in my life really had.

My plea didn't change anything. Within thirty minutes, I was sitting in a van, eliminated from the show. It hit me. I had no money. I was going back to mountains of unpaid bills. I'd just been dumped on national television and had seen my family for the first time in years, only for my brother to hurt me again. The future was terrifyingly bleak. Had I misunderstood what God wanted me to do? Was all of this for nothing?

As I sat in the back seat of the van, hopelessness and hurt washed over me in painful waves. I lost sight of the shore and sank in an ocean of grief.

It took some time to realize the truth. Sean wasn't right for me. There's no doubt about that. But God didn't bring me onto *The Bachelor* to marry Sean. He brought me onto *The Bachelor* to strengthen my faith by teaching me to trust his will over my life, even when the future was unknown.

At that point, sitting slump-shouldered in the van as it sped

down the highway, I thought my journey on *The Bachelor* was over. I was returning to the life I'd left behind, the one rife with bills marked past due and extra shifts at the bridal salon. Though I didn't know it at the time, that old life would soon be gone forever. My journey on *The Bachelor* was far from over and the best was yet to come.

SEVEN

BECOMING THE BACHELORETTE

Desiree Hartsock has reportedly been spotted
with a television crew—which would seem to
all but confirm she has finalized her contract
to be the next *The Bachelorette* star.

—*REALITY TV WORLD*

Y ou know those moments that define the rest of your life?
The way you handle situations, or the way you react and
respond? The memories that last forever? It's funny to look back
at many moments in my life as a young girl when I laughed in
the face of fear.

It was summertime, and my mom took us kids to the pool

for the day. I was just four years old and hadn't yet learned how to swim without my floaties. Growing up with an older brother, I naturally had to keep up and prove my capacity for life and adventure. Also, with an independent spirit and a no-holds-barred attitude, I was primed for a challenge. I remember it as clear as day. Toes slowly crept toward the edge of the water, shoulders back as I scanned the bustling pool full of kids of all ages. I slipped my floaties off moments prior so as not to bring attention to myself. I took one last look back at my mom sunbathing on her chair, not facing my direction. I knew I couldn't make this happen if she saw me, so I discreetly made my way to the other side of the pool. With no eyes on me, I jumped. *Splash!* I started kicking my feet and emulating the other swimmers' movements. I realized almost immediately that the ability of my body didn't match the belief in my mind and that I was about to drown. Thankfully it was only the shallow end. I opened my eyes underwater and grabbed onto an older girl swimming up to the stairs, which pulled me up to safety. She got mad at me because I accidentally scratched her in my attempt to live, but little did she know she was an angel.

While this experience as a young person was quite scary, the resiliency of a child is even greater. I continued to jump into pools until I learned how to swim and kept my floaties on until I was certain.

To this day, it's still mind-boggling to me that I was the star of *The Bachelorette*. It's a once-in-a-lifetime opportunity that only a handful of women receive, and it changes the very fabric of your reality. It's a role I stepped into without any understanding of the weight it would hold for my future. I jumped into the deep end without my floaties on, hoping Prince Charming would save me. While I learned you can't rely on a Prince Charming, I am thankful I trusted the process and allowed my faith and God's hand to keep me from drowning.

· · ·

I had just been eliminated by Sean and was coming down from an emotional journey when I received a call from one of the producers.

"There's a lot to figure out, and we're just gauging interest," he said. "But would you consider being the Bachelorette?"

Most women would have jumped at the chance, but I was hesitant. I was coming out of the confusing whirlwind of *The Bachelor* and realizing how it had sucked me away from real life and consumed every waking minute. My debt had grown and was waiting for me. I was still exhausted from the intense filming schedule and hadn't processed everything that had happened. I said, "I'll pray about it."

Another week went by, and I was asked to have dinner with a few VIPs from the show to discuss *The Bachelorette*. I let myself imagine it—a second chance at love, and this time I would be in control. The thought was alluring, but I made myself stay realistic. The other contenders had so much going for them: solid families, established careers, and extroverted personalities that bloomed under the gaze of the cameras. They all seemed like they were made for the role, so I knew I shouldn't get my hopes up, and I wasn't sure if I was ready to hop right back into another emotional journey. *Lord,* I prayed, *if this is something you want, you will make it happen.* Immediately, a sense of calm came over my heart, and I went on my way, figuring that at the very least, I'd gotten a fancy night out.

Pushing the conversation out of my mind, I returned to my former job at a bridal salon in Beverly Hills and was quickly consumed with the rhythms of my previous life and paying off my compiled debt.

In January, two months after filming ended, *The Bachelor* aired, and I was shocked by how many people watched it and how drastically it changed my life. The day after the premiere, I was at a grocery store looking at two-for-one chip deals—because, let's be honest, it was all I could afford—when a hand tapped me on the shoulder.

"Oh my God, it's you!" a woman said enthusiastically, trapping me in the aisle with her shopping cart. "I'm rooting for you. You and Sean are so cute together. Does he pick you? I won't tell anyone." Without pausing for me to answer, she whipped out her phone, swiped to the camera app, and shoved it in my confused, makeup-free face. "Smile!"

Getting stopped for selfies and hugs with fans became a new normal, and every Monday when an episode aired, there was an explosion of notifications on my social media as thousands of people discussed the show. Complete strangers dissected me, scrutinizing—and frequently hating on—everything from my clothes to the way I walked. I was called every name possible: boring, fun, authentic, disengaged, sweet, too sweet, not sweet enough. The bizarre fishbowl of attention—both good and bad— was a huge adjustment for me, an ordinary girl who hadn't even watched a full season of the show before.

Deep down, I wanted to be liked. Everyone does. And social media is a powerful tool that impacts all of us, whether it's on a big or small scale. It's tempting to use it as a metric for acceptance, reducing our value to the number of likes on our posts. I had to keep reminding myself that my identity was in God and not the comments section of an Instagram post. Social media can drown you, but knowing my true identity got me through. During filming, I had prayed every day that God's glory would be shown through me, and I prayed the same every day that a new episode aired. Praying helped me focus on what was important.

March came around and there was still no final word on who the next Bachelorette would be. I was on edge, anxious from having stood at this crossroads for so long without knowing which path would open. It was getting close to the end of *The Bachelor* season as I prepared for "The Women Tell All" episode. Still, I hadn't been officially offered the role, so I was nervous, especially since "The Women Tell All" episode is live and public speaking makes me want to die. I wiggled the fitted dress over my hips, and an assistant zipped it up. I stared into the full-length mirror, and insecurities rushed over me, driven by the voices I'd heard since the show aired. When I stepped out onto that stage, every single thing I did and said would be analyzed, and I was still raw from some of the things I'd read about myself online. I was tired from working so much, felt fat from those weeks of sitting around drinking wine in vacation rental homes, and didn't like the way the dress made my legs look (something I was constantly trolled about on social media). On top of all that, Mother Nature had paid me a visit, and I was terrified that I would leak through the filmy light fabric of the dress on national television. Talk about a bad headspace! But I said a silent prayer for peace, took a deep breath, and walked out onto that stage. God had gotten me that far, and if it was his will, I knew he would get me the rest of the way.

And, as we know, it was his will. "The Women Tell All" went smoothly, and within two weeks, the network officially offered me the role of Bachelorette. When I got the call, I marveled at how God had opened those doors for me. There was no doubt in my mind that he had ordered my steps. The other contenders had so much going for them. I was a young woman who didn't come from much and was largely alone in the world. Yet God had chosen me, and it's such a powerful example of the blessings that come when you seek his ways and not your own.

The next step before officially being announced as the new Bachelorette was the contract. It's difficult to put your worth in a dollar amount. Ultimately, a number can't determine our true worth or value, but as a Bachelorette, I felt that it did. "What do I deserve? What value do they see in me? Do I measure up to the past leads and what they were paid?" I had no metric to go off of, and you definitely can't trust Google. I knew that this opportunity was from the Lord and that no dollar amount would change my answer or the path I was on. But I did want to make it clear that while I could be humble, I could also be firm in a number that I felt any lead deserved. Any amount would have been more than enough to help me out of my current financial situation, and for that I was incredibly grateful.

It's small moments that change our lives forever. It's also how we respond to those situations that will keep us strong or make us weak. While I felt confident and strong leading up to the first night on *The Bachelorette*, in the moments that followed, I discovered that all I could rely on was God to get me through.

EIGHT

WHEN WHAT YOU WANT
ISN'T WHAT YOU NEED

Brooks Forester breaks up with Desiree Hartsock,
even though she admitted to being in love with him.

—*TODAY ONLINE*

Now we're back to the breakup with Brooks and my acceptance of Chris's marriage proposal. Those two actions
defined my season and sent the internet into a cacophonic uproar.

My actions make a lot more sense when seen in the context
of both Ryan and Andrew, yet they baffled viewers who didn't—
and couldn't—see that my relationships with Brooks and Chris
paralleled the struggles I had with my old and new self. The
world saw a steadily progressing relationship between Brooks and

me, and it was obvious that I was completely smitten with him. But they couldn't see what was going on behind the cameras and in my heart.

Let us start at the beginning. The first night of *The Bachelorette*, I stood in front of the Bachelor mansion, a jittery mess of nerves and excitement. My childhood self would laugh at the irony of me, an introvert, being the star of a TV show. But young Des would also be immensely proud of how far I had come. Chris Harrison placed me on my mark, and camerapeople set up in position.

Just as I finally felt ready to meet the guys, I heard bits of intense chatter coming from the headphones of the hair and makeup team. The hair stylist came forward, and she fluffed my hair and doused it with enough hair spray to make my head a fire hazard. I already didn't feel like myself, and when she continued a second and a third time to get my hair exactly right, uncertainties crept up. Did they think I wasn't pretty enough for this? Why did they keep fussing with my hair? Although it was all part of the role, the attention placed on my looks made me feel unsettled, especially since I—or my hair—was not giving them the look they wanted. I cared what the crew thought because they had worked with many other leads, and I wanted to make a good impression, not only with my suitors and the crew but also with the viewers. I knew this night would shape my identity as the Bachelorette.

Eventually, after several fluffing sessions and more hair-spray attacks, my hair was deemed acceptable, and the night got on its way.

Surreal is the only word I can use to describe the moment when the first limo pulled slowly into the courtyard with its cargo of hotties. I could still hardly believe they were all for me.

As anxious as I was, I knew those guys were even more so because their fates rested in my hands—er, roses. When I stepped out of the limo on *The Bachelor*, I worried about forgetting my name, but this time I worried about how I would remember the twenty-five names of my suitors!

. . .

Brooks was the second contestant out of the limo, and the minute he appeared, I knew I was in trouble—except I thought it was the fun, lose-your-heart-to-Prince-Charming kind of trouble, not repeat-the-patterns-from-your-past-and-get-completely-off-track trouble. The first thing that stood out to me was his hair, which had the tousled, debonair style you might find on the cover of a romance novel. It was just the sort that makes you want to run your hands through it.

"You look so stunning," he said to me. "Are you nervous? I'm nervous."

Brooks was a warm and genuine presence throughout a confusing and overwhelming night. The gimmicks were out in full force. One guy pranced around shirtless, while another took the opposite route and showed up in a suit of armor. So I had one guy who gave me quite an eyeful (to be fair, he had an actual eight-pack, so I was not complaining) and one guy where all I could see were his eyes through a slit in an armored helmet. And it wasn't simply fun and games. One contestant had one too many drinks and continually tried to get me into a DIY "fantasy suite." I thought I only had to worry about men trying to get me into dark places alone at a club, but no. Turns out dirtbags are also sometimes *Bachelorette* contestants. He made me extremely uncomfortable, and I ended up sending him home at once. No man should ever think a girl is only worth a dark, private room.

It was hard to decipher true personalities through the different facades that night or to even know who was there for the right reasons. But I did know that Brooks was extremely attractive and conversation with him was easy. I enjoyed his quirky personality and the way he put me at ease with his charm and humor. I knew I would be keeping him around.

• • •

Our first date was definitely a success. We had a great time dressing up like a bride and groom, eating cupcakes from a food truck, and driving along the coast in the Bentley I used during the show. Brooks was fascinating to me. He was a blast to hang out with, told funny stories, and was adventurous and spontaneous. Though I'd traveled a lot through Middle America with my family and a bit for *The Bachelor*, I'd never taken his types of trips. He explored the world to learn and have fun, and that was exactly what I wanted to do but never had the resources for. I loved the idea of being able to simply take off and go on a grand adventure because you'd stumbled across a cheap flight. For Brooks, it seemed as though the world was both his classroom and his playground, and his free spirit appealed to me.

I was swept away the moment we kissed for the first time on the Hollywood sign hillside.

I thought he had the two traits I knew I needed: expressiveness and a readiness to commit and get engaged. Neither was true. Instead, I confused compliments with communication and grand gestures with love.

After our Hollywood date, the next time I saw Brooks was at the cocktail party. He pulled me to the back of the Bachelor mansion. In a corner of the estate, he had painstakingly recreated the Hollywood sign with rocks. Be still my heart! The effort meant so much to me, and I felt like he was truly wooing me, something no guy had ever done before.

Whenever he saw me, he complimented me. Those gestures fed my soul, and I thought I had found someone who could communicate honestly and openly with me—someone who could finally talk to me about everything they were thinking and feeling. It wasn't until later that I realized the compliments were much more about how I looked than who I was.

"You look so nice," he would say. "I love it when you wear that dress."

As the show progressed, and contestants narrowed, cracks appeared in the veneer of our seemingly ideal relationship. I noticed Brooks was sensitive and would go through emotional highs and lows. I was okay with it because no one is perfect and you should accept people for who they are. If he was willing to work at our relationship, I could handle his moodiness. However, his insecurities only grew, and he began to question our relationship. I worked to reassure him and fight for us, just as I had with Ryan and Andrew. I didn't realize I was falling into old patterns from before. He was not ready for a committed relationship (at least not with me) but also wasn't being open and honest with me about it. Instead of talking to me, he retreated inward, and nothing I did could stop him.

Our fate was sealed on Brooks's hometown date in Salt Lake City, Utah. He was the last date of the four remaining contestants and had all week to think, without my reassuring or reminding him of what we had. In fact, in my predate interview clips, I said, "Brooks has been up and down this whole journey. I think he is maybe holding back from falling in love and letting himself go there, so I want him to just try to stay focused on what we have."

I arrived excited to spend time with him and meet his family. The daytime portion was spent canoeing at a park. Maybe it foreshadowed the rough waters ahead, but we had seafaring troubles and both got wet. After, we went to meet his family, which was so big that they give the Duggar family competition. (There were so many of them that they wore convention-style name tags so I could know who was who. Thanks, Foresters!)

When I talked privately with his mom and asked if Brooks was ready for an engagement, she said, "Yes, if he meets the right person."

It was the right thing to say, yet I could tell something lingered behind her response. I think she, and the rest of the family, couldn't see Brooks getting down on one knee and proposing at the end of the show. They had recently seen him go through a bad breakup and knew he wasn't ready to get engaged. In the footage where Brooks talks to his brothers, one says, "Do you think you can make Des happy for the rest of her life?"

To which he replies, "Good question."

When we stood in the driveway outside his family's home to say goodbye, I mentioned the conversation I had with his mother and how I'd asked if he was ready to be married. And I saw it: doubt. I saw it in his eyes, as readable and obvious as a billboard. I think, at that moment, he realized how real this was to me and that there was a whole life beyond the show that I might want with him. Even then he put me in a strange limbo of uncertainty. He didn't express love, nor did he share where he was at. I left confused about whether the show was simply wearing on him or if he really was questioning everything. Still, we'd come so far and gone through so much, and I had poured so much of my heart and soul into our relationship. He wouldn't just throw that all away, would he?

I thought we could overcome his doubts, but just one week later, I was crying on a dock in Antigua.

That day was so hard. The only thing I wanted was to be alone, but I still had an obligation and desire to show up for the other men still there.

Desperate for some space, I fled to the bathroom, locked the door, and got into the tub. My shoulders shook as I sobbed and hugged my knees to my chest. I couldn't ignore the truth any longer. I had lost Brooks, yes, but what hurt even more was realizing that I had lost myself again. I had worked so hard to undo the dark strands of my past and live in the knowledge that God loved and valued me—and because of that, I didn't need love from others to prove my worth. Yet I had been entangled in old patterns once again and fallen for the wrong guy. It seemed as though my efforts to be a different, better person were for nothing.

· · ·

Looking back, I have a much better understanding of what happened, and I hold so much more grace for myself than I did at the time. Up to that point, my whole life had been unstable. Brooks, with his spontaneity and love for adventure, spoke to the flighty part of me that never had a solid home and used distractions to fill the empty places in my heart. I don't think Brooks ever wanted to hurt me. He simply couldn't be what I needed, and I was so used to fighting for relationships that I couldn't see it. Sometimes when we fall for someone, we are blinded to the fact that we're trading our needs for what we think we want. In my case, I thought I wanted this creative, world-traveling, enigmatic guy when what I needed was someone strong, grounded, and confident in who they were. I needed someone who could anchor me, love me fearlessly, and pursue me while building a beautiful life together as best friends and lovers.

Thank the Lord there was someone there who was all of that and more. But first I needed to turn back to my God.

NINE

DRAMA KINGS

On *The Bachelorette*, the mind games continue
among Desiree Hartsock and her suitors.

—*THE LOS ANGELES TIMES ONLINE*

Before I get into the nitty-gritty of the Brooks fallout, let's
talk about the boys.

All of them.

It's a single girl's dream, right? Twenty-five gorgeous suitors
vying for your hand. What they don't tell you is that when you
take twenty-five guys and put them in a situation in which they
are striving to win the heart of one woman, you get more drama
than you'd find at a theatrical festival of Shakespeare tragedies.
Forget drama queens—drama kings is more like it! Egos and tes-
tosterone abounded, along with lots of man tears.

Before the show was cast, the producers asked me to break down my ideal Prince Charming so they could find guys I would naturally be drawn to.

My list was as follows:

Personality: person of faith, expressive, adventurous, spontaneous, funny, and grounded.

Physicality: brunette, athletic build, and no one under six feet tall (I'm five feet seven, and in heels can easily be six feet, so I wanted someone tall).

Casting really did their due diligence because any of the guys could have been a shirtless Abercrombie & Fitch model circa 2005. And beyond the defined jawlines, almost all the guys were sincere, earnest, and good-hearted.

People magazine asked me to give my first impression of each guy with one word. If you browse the list, I used *Ken doll, Superman, sweet, beefcake, smart, creative, outspoken,* and *athletic,* among several other adjectives (I'm sure you're wondering . . . for Brooks, I put *witty,* and for Chris, I put *handsome*). So I had an amazing selection overall. But even these sincere, earnest, and good-hearted guys had their breaking points.

Drama began on the first night with the aforementioned guy who thought it'd be a good idea to take me away to an upstairs room. I sent him home but unfortunately couldn't do the same with the drama—it only morphed and accelerated from there.

Just three weeks into filming, Chris Harrison called to inform me that one of the guys, Brian, had a girlfriend back home. I went to talk to Brian, and before I knew it, the girlfriend was striding across the courtyard and I was in the middle of a *Jerry Springer* episode in which Brian accused her of throwing rocks at his face and she called him a "lying, cheating, deceitful pig." There was no chance he was there for the right reasons—or that he was staying. I just wanted him out of the house and to put it all behind me.

I was lucky enough to have two main villains on my season (insert eye roll here). Their names were Ben and James. Ben didn't care about fame, but he also did not care about making friends. James had buddies in the house yet gave the impression that he wanted to be the next Bachelor. Though I can now enjoy some of the drama while watching new seasons of the show from the safety of my couch and with a glass of red wine, I'll always remember how intense it was to live through.

How did things shake out with these two? Let's start with Ben. He was a single dad who brought his young son to meet me that first night. (And, by necessity, Ben's mother, who took care of the toddler afterward. I met three generations in the space of five minutes! Looking back, I think having your prospective love interest meet both your mom and child at the same time they meet you might not be the best move.) I thought Ben's son was adorable and appreciated how Ben made it clear he was there for me. Unfortunately, he made it a little too clear by continually breaking in on my conversations with the other contestants. It didn't sit well with the guys, but to be fair to Ben, the guys were probably jealous because I gave him the first rose. Ben collected as many foes as he did roses. When we got to Germany, I chose him and another contestant, Michael, for the dreaded two-on-one date.

"This is going to be uncomfortable," I said in the predate interview, and truer words have never been spoken. All three of us were loaded into a hot tug, which is a hot tub–boat hybrid, and sent off across an icy lake. Unless one of us wanted to jump overboard and risk hypothermia, we were stuck on the world's most scenic yet most awkward date. It was clear that Michael, who is an attorney, did not like Ben and wanted nothing more than to see him go home. By the time we got to dinner, Michael had forgotten we were on a date and not in a courtroom and cross-examined Ben on his lack of faith (his prime evidence was the fact that Ben didn't go to church on Easter) and his parenting skills. I certainly didn't appreciate Michael badgering Ben, but I did know that Michael, as abrasive as he was, had my back and wanted to look out for me. I sent Ben home at the end of the date because I had reservations about him and our connection had been lost in the he-said/he-said drama.

I thought our experience in Barcelona would be filled only with sangria, flamenco, and dinner at nine o'clock from there on out, but on *The Bachelorette*, drama sprouts faster than Hydra heads. By then, lines had been drawn among the guys. Brooks and Michael were on one side and James was on his own, with the remaining men looking the other way and awkwardly taking sips from their drinks whenever arguments broke out. The two sides couldn't stand each other and also couldn't understand how I could genuinely like all three guys when they were so different.

We had a group date involving a soccer match, and the tension among the guys was thicker than the fog swathing the city every morning. It was my birthday, but it didn't feel like it. By the time we got to the nighttime portion, I was exhausted and felt torn in different directions. Everyone's emotions were heightened, and I constantly had to make big decisions with no reprieve in between. Every rose ceremony ended with goodbyes, and they were becoming more and more painful.

I was getting ready in the bathroom for the nighttime portion of the group date after the soccer game, and suddenly, I began to sob. I knew even more drama awaited me once I stepped outside the door, and it was simply too much. I didn't have anyone to talk to and sort through everything with, and the pressure and loneliness wore on me. I stifled my sobs and rushed to get ready, making sure my eyes didn't become too red and puffy for filming. Finally, I went out to spend time with the guys, but the night was as drama-filled as I feared. Kasey and Michael accused James of wanting to be the next Bachelor and date other women, creating tangible tension in the group.

Chris was my saving grace that night. He took me upstairs to an abandoned bedroom. We lay on the bed, propped up on our elbows like we were high school sweethearts. Amid the chaos of the night, it was the one stabilizing moment, and for a brief time, I found equilibrium. He didn't bring up the division among the guys, and we talked about us, not anything else.

Eventually, I had to return to the "party," and as I walked down the stairs, I cringed at the angry shouts echoing through the old building. The guys were rallying the troops in an effort to get James eliminated, and pretty much everyone was on board. I tend to think about how things are affecting everyone else, and I made my decision for the peace of all involved. I actually liked James quite a bit. We had a great connection and natural chemistry, and I think his comments about wanting to be the next Bachelor were taken out of context. Whenever we were together, we had a great time, and he was incredibly attractive. But his presence was causing problems, particularly for Brooks, who began to question my judgment. Since I couldn't see myself marrying James, I decided to let him go for the sake of everyone, James included.

Oddly enough, I also had the good fortune of having a future

Bachelor on my show: Juan Pablo, the handsome, former pro soccer player from Miami. People often ask me about him and my time with him. I was definitely attracted to him—who wouldn't be? He's a gorgeous human specimen with crystal-clear green eyes and a dashing smile. And, of course, his Spanish accent was enough to make me swoon every time he talked about his daughter and whispered sweet nothings in Spanish in my ear (I'm not complaining about that; sweet nothings sound even better in Spanish). We just didn't have much to build on. Personally, I never experienced any of the behavior he exhibited on his season, and he stayed out of the drama in mine, so I was a little surprised to see that other side of him—and glad I didn't have to deal with it because I had my hands full as it was.

I am often asked about Juan Pablo, Brooks, Ben, Chris, and James along with one other man: Chris Harrison, the face of Bachelor Nation itself. Whenever people ask about him, I always have the sense that they hope he's as genuine as he seems on screen. I'm happy to report he is. He was always professional and kind, and I'm glad he was there. Watching more recent seasons, I've enjoyed seeing more of his personality shine through.

To say my season was intense is an understatement. There was somehow more drama per capita than there were contestants! But the darkest low still awaited me.

You might be thinking I mean the breakup with Brooks. And that was awful and painful and as dramatic as could be. But a whole second wave of drama occurred long after the show was done filming, one that shook the very foundation of my life. It came as the show aired, and even though I'd experienced a taste of public scrutiny from doing *The Bachelor*, I was blown away by the severity of public backlash over the breakup with Brooks and my engagement to Chris. Even going to the grocery store was stressful because I didn't know what someone might say to me or what the tabloid headlines would read at the checkout. I think people forget that even though someone is on a TV show, they are still a real person with genuine feelings. Nothing is more shattering than to be misunderstood, judged, and criticized by strangers. Every cruel word echoed the hurtful things I heard growing up.

Whenever you engage online, I encourage you to think before you type. Harsh words are hurtful in both directions—damaging not only the heart of the recipient but the heart of the sender as well. So be gracious and kind!

TEN

THE RULES OF
ENGAGEMENT

Bachelorette recap: Is Desiree going to end up alone?

—THE LOS ANGELES TIMES ONLINE

I don't know how long I sat in the porcelain shelter of the bath-tub after Brooks's unexpected exit in Antigua. I do know I didn't climb out until I was sure the cameraman had left, because I couldn't bear the thought of being filmed anymore. Taking a shaky breath, I clamored out of the bath and went into my bed-room. One of the producers came to talk with me and make sure I was doing okay. Of course, I wasn't, but I appreciated the senti-ment. Finally, she left and I climbed into my bed (I may or may not have had a bottle of wine with me at this point). Everything

was quiet except for the far-off sound of the ocean and a soft breeze stirring the branches outside my window.

There, in the stillness, I knew what I had to do. One of the few personal items you can bring on the show is a Bible, and I opened mine, my eyes desperately running over the verses printed across the thin pages. As I read God's Word, a surge of hope filled my soul.

The Bachelorette is a bewildering alternate universe that is all-consuming. Many voices surround the stars of the show. The guys say all manner of things to secure their spots and get your attention. And there are the voices yet to come—once the show began to air, I knew my face would be splashed across tabloids, my actions would be used as comedic fodder for late-night television, and my most vulnerable moments would be parsed apart in 280-character captions across the Twitterverse.

With these other voices in my head, I failed to hear the one that mattered most—the still, small voice. I always wanted discernment and clarity, but somewhere along the way, I began to rely on my own feelings rather than seeking God's direction.

I cried out to God from my bed that night, and his presence settled over my heart. I was his, and he was working everything together for my good, even yet another heartbreak.

One of the most powerful things about the Christian life is that it's not a single moment or a one-and-done encounter with God. It's a journey, one taken step-by-step, and it's full of both missteps and victories. I had gotten off track, yet the minute I called out to him, he was there, an ever-present help in times of trouble, exactly as the Bible says.

Hope came to me through Jeremiah 29:11, which says, "'For I know the plans I have for you,' declares the Lord, 'plans to

prosper you and not to harm you, plans to give you hope and a future.'"

The hope I'd had while filming *The Bachelor*—that the best was yet to come—returned. I had peace for the first time in a long time, even as my heart hurt and my eyes were still red and puffy from sobbing.

The next morning, I considered what I should do and whether a future existed for me on the show. I had a few options.

1. I could choose no one and leave the show single. I already knew how viewers would see the breakup with Brooks and that most would assume there was no way I could genuinely move on with anyone else. No one would be surprised if I ended things with Chris and Drew, packed my bags, and headed home as a newly minted member of the Lonely Hearts Club. It would be a far cry from the fairy tale I always wanted, but no one could fault me.

2. I could stay and spend the remaining time exploring things further with Chris and Drew. As dazzled as I'd been by Brooks, Chris—the mysterious, poetic baseball player from Seattle, Washington—had snuck into my heart from the very beginning. My relationship with Drew had a slow start but had immense potential if we had more time. If things kept progressing the way I thought they might and I kept having peace about it, I could accept a proposal from one of these guys at the end (if he offered one). But if I did, it would not be pretty. No one would understand. Viewers would accuse me of rebounding or settling, and it would be a scandal unlike anything in the *Bachelor* archives.

3. Alternatively, if things went well between us and I wanted to save myself from the judgment of viewers, I could tell the final guy I simply wanted to date. We could quietly head off into the sunset and then, when things settled down, get engaged once a healthy amount of time separated us from the show and everyone had moved on.

I never seriously considered the first option. I was drawn to both Chris and Drew, but I had a sense Chris and I could go all the way. He'd been my rock through the whole season, and our relationship was different from any I'd ever had. I was torn between the second two options, and I emotionally ping-ponged back and forth between them.

The next two weeks of filming gave me a lot of intentional time with Chris, and I soaked it up like a flower deprived of the sun. From the beginning, he'd been a presence so strong and steady that it scared me. Now I dug deeper with him, all the while praying about our relationship and reading the Bible regularly.

God, is this the one you have for me? I prayed. *If Chris gets down on one knee, should I accept a proposal? Is it your will for us to be together?*

At this point I couldn't imagine ever saying goodbye to him. We went together like two peas in a pod, and the more time we spent together, the more my heart filled with a love I never knew. As I continued to pray about it, the more certain I became. Chris was the one God had for me. He was the "best" that was yet to come.

And there was one other thing that confirmed our relationship—something only I knew about.

Before the show, I had started seriously seeking the Lord, attending church regularly, and spending devoted time praying, Bible reading, and journaling. I became friends with a bridal-stylist-in-arms named Sarah, and we were on similar journeys of renewing our faith.

One day, as I was meditating on Bible verses and journaling my thoughts, I jotted down the word *Oregon*. I'd never been to the state and didn't know anyone there. My only point of reference for it was the fact that Portland is a breeding ground for hipster singer/songwriters and it's where the *Twilight* movies were filmed. I knew trees and fog were a thing there (an impression I may or may not have also gotten from *Twilight*). Still, the word *Oregon* wouldn't leave my mind, and I wondered if the Lord was drawing me there for a reason. Interestingly, Sarah, completely on her own, had the same urge toward this state.

I hadn't thought about Oregon since starting the show until I was flying to Chris's hometown date— and realized it was in Oregon! I'd always thought of Chris in terms of Seattle because that's where he lived. I immediately thought about my prayer journal and how I had written about Oregon.

Chris was born and raised in McMinnville, Oregon, a small town located about two hours from the nearest airport. My plane landed, and the air was crisp, unlike the smoggy, polluted air of Los Angeles. Towering trees lined the roads, and behind those sat a stunning range of mountains. The drive to McMinnville was enchanting. From my window, I watched as verdant farmland gave way to the quaint neighborhoods of Chris's childhood town. I've always loved nature and had never seen anything like this.

Since the drive was two hours long, it was the first time in a while I was able to rest and hear myself think. In the rare moment of quiet, a whisper flowed over me, and it was so strong and clear that it had to have been from the Lord.

You belong here.

I believe God speaks to us in a variety of ways, and this was one of the ways he spoke to me. Even before I'd met Chris, God was preparing my heart. (This was also how he spoke to Sarah. Believe it or not, both of us ended up married to guys named Chris from Oregon. Spiritual twinning!) God was preparing my own heart, but for the entire year leading up to *The Bachelor*, I prayed for the Lord to prepare my future husband's heart as well. I would plead, "I may not know who he is, but when I meet him, let him be ready for me."

When I arrived, Chris greeted me with a bouquet of wildflowers he'd picked on his way to see me. It was as though he'd collected some of Oregon's beauty and placed it into my hands for me to keep. He also gave me a dandelion to make a wish. As its feathery head disassembled and floated away under my breath, I was happy. Hand in hand, we walked to the baseball diamond where he spent years learning to play. Chris played minor league baseball before an injury forced him to retire, and then he became a mortgage lender. You can see why I fell for him—my babe has brawn and brains! I impressed Chris with my batting skills, and I'll have you know I hit a homer off of him.

Eventually, we settled down on blankets atop the pitcher's mound, and with his arms wrapped around me, I gave him a gift. The whole time we'd been dating, I'd been filling a sketchbook with drawings of our special times together and, in a stroke of literary inspiration, had named each one something cute, like *Rooftop Rendezvous*. Shakespeare has nothing on my word game!

We went to meet his family, and they were an extension of Chris: grounded, genuinely amazing people who welcomed me with open arms and hearts. His dad is a chiropractor and even gave me an adjustment, so I left with an aligned spine and the sense that I could belong—not just in Oregon but with them, Chris's family.

. . .

With Brooks out of the picture, and after spending dedicated time with Chris, I was completely in love . . . and utterly conflicted because I knew that if I left the show with Chris's ring on my finger, the wrath of the entertainment blogosphere would descend on me.

The easiest thing to do would be to date and get engaged later. But as I sought God and spent time with Chris, I knew the only reason I would put off a proposal was out of fear—fear of what people would think and say about me. Because of my past and lack of self-confidence, I never spoke up for what I needed—not with Chris and not in past relationships (heck, not even with Brooks!). Looking back, I saw God's divine intervention and timing. I needed to experience Brooks's leaving to let go of my toxic relationships, to shed my past, and to become a woman who could love another because she knew God loved her.

I also saw that choosing Chris and being open to an engagement was another step in the growth of my faith. I couldn't let myself live in fear of the judgment of others any longer, no matter how hard it might become, especially not when I knew I was doing the right thing.

By faith, I decided that I would say yes if Chris proposed.

ELEVEN

HESITATIONS, NO MORE

So as you go through this journey,
Along emotional roads not straight, but curvy.
Remember I'm here and I'm thinking of you,
And the thought of us now is ever so true!

—*"HESITATIONS, NO MORE"*

These are lines from a poem Chris
wrote to me during the show.[2]

This is my favorite love story. It's the true fairy tale that I didn't even realize was happening at first. It begins like this.

Once upon a time, a professional-baseball-player-turned-mortgage-lender moved to Seattle, Washington. His name was

Chris Siegfried, and he was settling into his new home and job, so his love life wasn't a priority at the moment. It could wait, he figured, until he had his ducks in a row.

One day he was walking around with a friend when fate intervened in the form of Cupid disguised as a casting agent for *The Bachelorette*. The agent waved him down and said, "You're the type of guy we're looking for. Would you be interested in being on *The Bachelorette*?"

"Does it pay?" Chris asked sensibly (you can tell he works in finance!).

To which the agent said, "Well . . . no. But you can get a free vacation out of it!"

On the spot, Chris declined. That would've been it, but his friend, sensing that these types of opportunities don't come along often, got the agent's card.

Later that evening, Chris happened to mention the encounter to his roommate and his roommate's fiancée. While Chris was *Bachelor* illiterate and had never seen a single season, his roommate's fiancée was a fan and exclaimed, "This is huge! No way can you pass this up. You're single—what do you have to lose?"

Chris decided that maybe, just maybe, this could be an interesting adventure. He got the card from his friend and went to a casting event in Los Angeles. After he was cast, he figured he should do his due diligence and watch Sean's season to see the contenders for *The Bachelorette*. He called his mom and said, "If it's Des, I really want to go."

. . .

The first thing I thought when Chris stepped out of the limo on the first night of *The Bachelorette* was that he was extremely handsome—talk about tall, dark, and handsome with emphasis on the tall (Chris is six feet four)—but also that he might be too clean-cut for my taste.

He crossed the courtyard, and when I saw how nervous he was, my heart melted a little. It was endearing that this tall, handsome guy who had every natural right to be confident was nervous to meet me. But he defied my expectations by busting out the most memorable introduction of the night.

He said, "There's something I really need to do. Do you mind . . ."

"What?" I asked as he dropped to one knee, proposal style. *Where is he going with this?*

". . . if I tie my shoe?"

I burst out laughing and then laughed even harder when he stood up and said, "I'm glad we can get off on the right foot."

The pickup line and the pun completely reframed my mindset on him. Right there, in that courtyard, I knew he had the exact same type of weird humor as I do. As I watched him walk into the Bachelor mansion, I actually editorialized and said, "He's funny."

I knew right away he was someone I wanted to know better.

• • •

My second memory of Chris was at a pool hangout at the Bachelor mansion. The last I'd seen him, he'd been wearing a formal suit at the cocktail party on the first night. Now he emerged from the mansion in swim trunks. My reaction? Jaw meet floor. I'd thought he was a lean guy, but I was mistaken. The boy had abs and muscles for days. The main producer and I were both taken aback by this hottie with a body.

Group dates always revealed so much about the guys. I got to see who was determined to pursue me, which guys would simply give up and become very attractive wallpaper, and how everyone interacted in a group setting. Let me tell you—on the dodgeball date, Chris was the star. And not because of his amazing athleticism (though watching him dominate the court didn't hurt). It was because no matter where I was, I found myself drawn to his gaze. Our eyes would meet, and he would give a subtle nod that said, *I'm here.* Many guys continually jockeyed for position and always tried to sit next to me or stay physically near me. I couldn't turn around without bumping into one of them. Chris never engaged in any of those power plays, yet without having to be at my side, still communicated that he was there for me. His confidence and self-assurance were beyond attractive.

Later on that night, Chris pulled me aside and said he wanted to show me something. I let out a sigh of relief. It was nice to have a moment without a guy walking up and asking, "Do you mind if I steal you?" as though I were the Hope Diamond. We went up an elevator and then climbed a flight of stairs. A door was at the top, and he held it open for me. I stepped through it, gasping at the view of the Los Angeles cityscape. Skyscrapers surrounded us on all sides, their glass exteriors reflecting the night sky like mirrors. Far below, headlights from cars cast long shadows that danced across the streets.

Sitting down, we talked, and everything was so . . . beautifully normal. It was like sucking in air after holding your breath for too long. Our conversation was natural and easy, and I was intrigued by Chris. He wasn't trying to say the right thing—instead, he was legitimately getting to know me. I'd forgotten what it was like simply to be seen for who I was, not the rose I could offer.

I didn't want our time to end, so when we were back with the rest of the guys, I gave him the night's rose. Everyone else left, and in true *Bachelorette* style, a singer came out to serenade us while we danced. It was intended to be a fantasy, but we pretended our date was just the opposite—that it was ordinary—and that made it all the more magical.

We created a fictional story line where Chris had picked me up at a bar and we'd stumbled upon a street musician. In our alternate reality, there were no cameras, mics, or producers. It was just us, and for a brief moment, lingering in the moonlight, I could pretend it was true. That's when he pulled me in close and we kissed for the first time.

Now, I'm not complaining about the kiss. The technical execution was a ten, but he pulled away after a few moments and simply held me. I was used to the guys flinging themselves into make-out sessions with such intensity that you'd think they were searching for my tonsils. I didn't think he was doubting our relationship, so I knew his restraint stemmed from something else. I decided it would be worthwhile to wait and find out just what was going on with this guy.

I saw Chris again at yet another group date. This one was in Atlantic City, and the guys were competing in a spoof Mr. America competition. I got to see Chris's goofy side when he went straight for a pair of high heels and paraded around in them with a panache that would make RuPaul proud. I couldn't stop laughing.

Nothing ever got to Chris. He was confident but not arrogant, and he never pressured me for reassurances or asked me how I felt about him. Instead, he simply shared his heart with me, despite that I was dating many other guys.

After the Atlantic City group date and the accompanying rose ceremony, he privately gave me a framed poem. He had written it himself. It was called "Hesitations, No More" and shared just that—that he was here for me, no hesitations whatsoever.

Chris was never fully comfortable around the cameras. He was always aware of them and cognizant of how he came across. It may sound odd that I liked this about him, but it showed me that he wasn't there for the fame or to gain Instagram followers. I don't think the full range of his witty, fun-loving, quick-tongued personality was captured on the show, so viewers didn't understand how much I was falling for him. I appreciated his authenticity, though, because it proved he wanted to make sure he represented his family well and that he was there for only one reason—me.

As for me, I knew I liked him, but I kept waiting for a curveball. "He's too perfect," I told myself over and over. There were no problems with him, and that precisely became the problem. When the other relationships on the show had difficulties, I could jump in and try to fix them as I had in my past. I'd never had a steady, healthy relationship, and Chris's maturity and open communication was, ironically, setting off my alarm bells.

We got to Germany for a new set of dates, and I couldn't wait to have a one-on-one date with Chris. But it did not start off well. I was jet-lagged and PMSing with debilitating cramps. I woke up at three o'clock in the morning and couldn't fall back asleep. I had to get up early because we needed to film B-roll of me wandering around the city before my date with Chris. To wake up, I drank a whole pot of coffee, underestimating just how strong the German brew would be. Soon I was completely awake but very jittery, over-caffeinated, and nauseous from the cocktail of cramps and coffee. I felt absolutely horrible, with no time to fully get in the mood for filming. The morning air was frigid, and I had to traipse around like I was the living embodiment of *Eat Pray Love.*

By the time Chris arrived, I was caffeine-crashing, cold, and exhausted, a perfect trifecta of misery.

But once I saw his beaming face, I was reset. Turns out love is an effective cure-all for crankiness—and even getting dumped. Oh, did I mention what happened on our date? One of the guys, Bryden, showed up while Chris and I were dancing around the public square. Bryden pulled me aside to tell me he was leaving. I was startled and confused. My interview, which happened right after Bryden's poorly timed exit, shows what Chris meant to me. I said, "It hurts. But I'm not going to let Bryden affect my date with Chris. Not at all. I just want to get back to Chris so I can feel happy again."

Chris was a balm to my heart, and the minute I was back with him, everything was good again. Like any other couple abroad, we explored the city and soaked up the local culture. We ate bratwursts and drank beer and tried on lederhosen, which made us look like Von Trapp children. As we strolled hand in hand through the cobblestone streets, I imagined, for the first time, what life would be like with Chris by my side.

Later we dined in a castle, and despite the stunning ceilings that arched above us and the beautifully styled table, I only had eyes for him.

Chris told me, "I'm ready to start a family and build a new life."

Nothing could've made me happier. What we were building on was something tangible and true, and when a guy discusses future plans with you, you know he's taking the relationship seriously. Our momentum continued into our date in Antigua a few weeks later. Things were getting serious. There were only three guys left, but as I lay in Chris's arms, with his hands tangled in my hair, I was at peace.

．　．　．

At dinner, Chris told me we needed to talk through certain things. And he didn't want to talk only about himself. He wanted to talk about me and, most importantly, us. When I saw the nervousness in his eyes, my immediate thought was that he was having doubts, and I was immediately scared. But it was the opposite. Chris wanted to have a transparent conversation about how we would work once the show was over and we were back in the real world. He'd just started his job in Seattle and was wondering if I would move there. Together, we weighed the pros and cons, and since I didn't have roots anywhere and already felt pulled to the Pacific Northwest, I told him I was open to moving to Seattle. It was an authentic conversation about the real types of challenges every couple faces. As we talked, I felt a deep sense of respect for Chris. He wanted us to have a strong foundation to build a life on, and he was already looking into the future and seeing us together. A question I get asked often is whether I talked about my faith with the guys during the show. I talked about my faith with many of the guys and especially with the remaining four guys; it just was never aired. The faith conversation I had with

Brooks in Spain on our date actually made me doubt his ability to be the kind of future husband I had hoped for. But as many women do, I brushed those thoughts aside for the time being to see if those doubts would change. With Chris, he solidified the feelings I had regarding my faith and the kind of Christ-centered relationship I wanted to have in a marriage. Although he grew up with a Catholic background and I with a Pentecostal Christian background, he was extremely supportive and excited to share his belief in God. This made me hopeful and excited to imagine a future with him.

. . .

Let's get back to the romance. One thing I didn't mention about Chris's hometown date in McMinnville, Oregon, was our kiss. You'll remember Chris and my first kiss was great but restrained while dancing in the moonlight on his first group date. As we got to know each other better, I noticed that Chris was tremendously respectful and a complete gentleman when it came to our physical interactions. He was reassuring in every other area, so I suspected he was waiting to make sure we would go the distance before getting more expressive with kissing. In hindsight, I think Chris's restraint was more than being worried about his mom clutching her pearls. Chris wanted to put the emotional safety of our hearts before immediate physical gratification. It showed wisdom and discernment on his part, even though I wasn't used to it.

The hometown date went so well, and before I knew it, it was time to say goodbye and climb into the van that waited to take me to my next destination. We relished our last few moments together and sat on a bench outside his family's home. Suddenly, he looked at me with an intensity I'd never seen from him before. He pulled me close and kissed me with such abandon and fierceness that I lost my breath. Gone was the restraint. It was like he'd decided that no matter what, he was mine and I was his and that was all that mattered. We were able to kiss for only a few minutes before I had to go, but those minutes were the most blissful taste of eternity I've ever had. When we had to part, my lips were numb and my heart raced. I knew he was all in.

Chris's hometown date was right before my hometown date with Brooks, and I felt torn. I understand now: I was warring between my old and new self. I wish I could've made the right decisions from that moment on. I wish I had sent Brooks home and embraced all Chris offered me. Sadly, that wasn't the case. Not yet.

Still, even though turbulence was ahead, our kiss on the bench outside Chris's childhood home was a glimpse into the good ultimately awaiting me and the fact that, when everything was said and done, it would be he and I—hesitations, no more.

TWELVE

I JUST WANT TO GO HOME (ONLY NOT REALLY)

The Bachelorette decided to soldier on and
hold a rose ceremony with the two remaining
men: Drew Kenney and Chris Siegfried.

—*E! ONLINE*

There is no rest for the weary, especially when you're the star of a television dating show. Though a wonderful life with Chris awaited me, I had to get there first. After Brooks departed, Chris wasn't the only one left. Drew also remained. So the very next day after Brooks left, I had to go right into a rose ceremony with Chris and Drew.

Chris Harrison arrived early to discuss what had happened.

I'd already spent the night praying and reading my Bible. I was spiritually re-centered, but the emotions from the breakup were still raw. The crew spoke to me in soft voices and looked at me with concerned expressions as though I were bereaved. Chris and I sat down on the patio, and the cameras began filming.

He looked at me with sympathy and gravely asked, "How are you doing?"

Well, in reality, I was fine. I'd given the events of the past twenty-four hours to the Lord and was ready to move forward into what he had for me. But, of course, the minute someone asks you how you are after a traumatic event, you break down. Tears coursed down my cheeks, and I dabbed futilely at them.

"Here's the more important question." Chris paused, drawing the moment out. "What do you want to do now?"

Full-on crying, I said the infamous sentence that everyone would latch on to once the episode aired. Between quavering breaths, I said, "I just want to go home, to be honest."

• • •

It is funny to write this part after the previous chapter. As it was, my heart was on its way to its real home. One which would start with Chris and grow to include two beautiful boys and a fur baby. The "home" I had at that time was a sparsely furnished studio apartment in Santa Monica, and there was nothing homey about it. I didn't actually want to go there or leave the show. I had already decided I was staying on the show and wanted to see it through. What I wanted was simply a hug and to be told that everything would be okay. I was away from my friends and everything that was known and familiar, so when I said I wanted to "go home," it was spoken from the part of me that just needed reassurance and a pint or two of cookie dough ice cream.

"Chris and Drew are still here for you," Chris said. "Could you see yourself with either of them?"

I already knew the answer. My heart was broken but my spirit wasn't, and I could see a future here. I said yes.

I tried to collect myself as Chris walked me to the rose ceremony site. Drew and Chris stood there, side by side. Obviously, Brooks wasn't present, and I wanted to be up-front and honest with my two remaining men. I told them that Brooks was gone and said, "It turned my world upside down. I don't want Brooks leaving to affect my relationship with you guys, and I won't let yesterday break my spirit." I reached for one of the two roses and continued. "Please, if you don't want to, just let me know."

They both came forward without any hesitation, and their confidence overwhelmed me. I looked at them and realized I was staring at two strong, caring, thoughtful men who loved me. How could I be upset? I almost felt ashamed that I'd spent so much emotional energy on Brooks. They stood on either side of me. The minute my eyes met Chris's, I felt a gravitational pull of my heart toward his, and I sank into his arms. I quickly stepped back because I wanted to be respectful to Drew, but I will always remember the strength of Chris's embrace.

. . .

Due to the intensity of the Brooks breakup, the producers suggested I take a few more days before the guys met my family and I went on a final date with each of them. I was glad to do so.

Drew's date came first, and we rode horses, plodding along

a trail that threaded through the Antigua hills. Just beyond the hills, the pristine blue ocean spread its vastness to the horizon. I, though, couldn't enjoy the tranquil surroundings. Before we embarked on the date, I had thought long and hard on our possible future and came to a decision. Like all the decisions before, this one was emotionally draining but seemed particularly intense, given how much time we'd spent together and how much I cared for him. Drew has the kindest heart and most gentle spirit I had ever come across. To hurt him when he was least expecting it felt unbearable. My heart was as heavy as the horses' hooves clomping along the dirt path.

"I can't even focus on this amazing view because I'm figuring out what I need to say to Drew," I told the cameras during an in-the-moment interview. "I need to tell him exactly how I'm feeling right now."

. . .

From the start, our relationship was promising. Beneath Drew's baby-blue eyes, model-status facial structure, and perfectly fitted shirts was a kind soul. He was a digital marketing analyst from Scottsdale, Arizona, and his sweet temperament was always a breath of fresh air. Throughout the show, he was open and honest. And in Spain, I got to see that there was some sexiness to go with that sweetness when he pushed me up against the wall and kissed me quite, ahem, thoroughly. But every time we were together, our interactions were serious. I kept wanting to see if he could let loose, have fun, and be spontaneous. I was certain that side existed, yet I never got to see it for myself. When I compared our journey with the parallel one I was having with Chris,

I was much further along with Chris. I wanted to give Drew and my relationship as much of a chance as possible, but as we rode through the Antigua foothills, I knew we were still figuring each other out and that he wasn't ultimately my husband.

It was only fair to send him home, and as the realization settled over me, unrelenting dread came with it. A mere two days earlier, I'd been dumped by Brooks and experienced the crushing confusion from being blindsided. Now I was about to be the one doling out the hurt, and everything in me didn't want to, especially when Drew had been so consistent and wonderful through the craziness that is *The Bachelorette*.

We reached our picnic spot and dismounted our horses. Big blankets and throw pillows awaited us, along with fruity alcoholic beverages in colorful tumblers. It looked like a set for a Pottery Barn catalog, not the grim location of a blindsiding breakup. We settled down next to each other, and Drew poured our tropical cocktails. Looking directly at me, he lifted his glass and said, "To being madly in love. And wanting to be nowhere else than here, with you."

Oh no! was my first thought. There's nothing more romantic than a handsome, wonderful guy professing his love to you . . . except when you don't reciprocate it and know you have to break his heart. I had to stop him right away. Quickly, I set down my glass.

"I really need to talk to you," I said. "Especially after that."

Immediately, Drew's face sobered. With the hardship of the past few days, the tears I hadn't been able to stop shedding began to flow again. But I wasn't crying for myself this time. I was crying for what I was about to do to this great guy who'd shown me genuine love and kindness.

I kept going. "I guess I don't even know where to start. It's just that the past couple of days have been a struggle with my heart and my mind, and I'm at this point that . . . I'm really reflecting and thinking about everything that has been leading up to this time. I would be so lucky—" I almost couldn't keep going as I saw the bewilderment and hurt that settled across his face. "I'd be so lucky to have you in my life but . . ."

And, of course, because Drew is such a good guy, he tried to comfort *me* and said, "It's all right."

But it wasn't all right. I kept going, trying to be open and share exactly where I was at because I remembered how confused I was after Brooks left.

"I don't know if I see our futures together. I just feel like there's something missing."

Then he said the words that stabbed my heart because they were the exact words I thought when Brooks told me he was leaving.

"I didn't see this happening."

"I never in a million years ever wanted to hurt you," I said, desperate to make things better, all the while knowing nothing would. "I just know."

"I guess I have to thank you for being honest," he said, still being such a gentleman. Then the confusion broke through and he said, "I don't know—what . . . I don't know . . . I don't know."

"I'm so sorry."

"You don't have to be sorry."

"I am, though." It was true. From the bottom of my heart, I meant it, and I wanted him to know. "You've been so honest and showed me that you care, and I've been hoping I could be the one to show you the love you deserve. It hurts me."

Drew took a long breath, and when he spoke again, finality and acceptance resonated in his voice.

"You don't have to be sorry for not being in love with me. It's not something you control. Just because I see it doesn't mean that you have to see it the same way. I would want you to be as in love with me as I am in love with you. This hurts . . . and it hurts a lot. I don't know when it'll really sink in but, um . . . I guess, uh, this is goodbye."

With that, he embraced me, and his hand wove through my hair. It was the sort of last hug that you never forget. From the first time he stepped out of the limo to that last moment together at our picnic, he was nothing but kind and gracious, and I'm better for having known him.

. . .

Later that evening, I was back in my bungalow and writing in my journal when it hit me. Chris was the only one left. An exhilarating sense of freedom came over me. It seems ideal to have twenty-five men to choose from, but in all reality, you don't want all twenty-five guys. You want to give your heart to one. To be truly known by one. While I enjoyed getting to know the other men throughout the duration of my season, it was a relief to have made it this far, narrowing it down to "the one." I'm grateful for the show because it brought me the love of my life, but I know how hard it can be on the hearts of those involved.

Since I was down to Chris, things felt normal (well, as normal as they can be on reality TV with a bevy of crew and cameras)—it was just me and the guy I loved. It was as though I'd been carrying around the heavy weight of everyone else's emotions and suddenly I could cast it aside. I was borderline ecstatic. The upcoming week would be just the two of us, and I wouldn't have to worry about splitting time fairly among the guys or making sure everyone got the reassurances they needed.

I could simply *be*.

Be loved. Be understood. Be free.

The hard part was that I would still be on verbal lockdown. I could bask in Chris's love and the fact that we were the only two left, but as far as he was aware, things would be business as usual. In my mind and heart, we were boyfriend and girlfriend, on the brink of engagement, but in Chris's mind he was still in a nonexclusive relationship. There was also still so much more to come, like meeting my family and deciding if he even wanted to propose. That is a lot for anyone. But if anyone could do it, it was Chris. His confidence and steadfastness made me fall in love with him, and it was those exact attributes that carried us all the way to the finale.

That week, I went on a date with him, and it was so freeing. All I could think was, "I don't want to let go of this man." The only time Brooks crossed my mind was after Chris and I had gone our separate ways. I was in my bungalow and reflecting on the past week. The thought of Brooks instantly brought me sadness—sadness because I'd spent so much time pursuing the wrong guy and looking for love in the wrong place. I even told the cameras, "I feel guilty for not having loved Chris from the beginning."

Even though I was now doing the right thing for me, a sinister sense of guilt tried to sneak into my heart. I think it's common—when we are set free from the lies of our past, new ones try to take their place. I had to stay in prayer, surrender that guilt to

God, and accept his grace. I make mistakes. We all do. And when we give them over to God, something powerful happens. He takes them, redeems them, and turns them into roads that lead us forward into his all-perfect plans. For me, he used the relationship and breakup with Brooks to show me I really was worthy of true love. Otherwise, shackled by my deeply ingrained patterns, I wouldn't have been able to move forward with Chris. God used that blindsiding breakup to show me true love and put me on the path to my true home.

THIRTEEN

MEET THE HARTSOCKS

Chris meets Desiree's family. Yep, including Nate.

— *DIGITAL SPY*

Many might think that as the Bachelorette the hardest part is deciding on which guy to get engaged to at the end. While that is quite challenging, the biggest hurdle for Chris and me to overcome once he was the only guy left was for him to meet my family. Nate in particular.

Despite this final hurdle, I was in a good space. Chris and I were progressing just as I hoped we would. I'd even managed to block out fears about the judgments yet to come once the show aired. I was continually reading my Bible and praying. In many ways, I was in the peaceful eye of a hurricane. I'd been tossed about by the torrential winds of *Bachelorette* drama, and more were yet to come, but for the time being, I was at peace. Mostly. Since Chris was meeting my family, he would also be meeting my brother. And we all saw how well that went with Sean.

. . .

After my hometown dates with all four guys, my brother came to town to discuss how things were going.

I hadn't seen my brother since my date with Sean, and since I didn't know how he felt about the show now, I was nervous about what he would say. And I didn't want my brother to meet any of the remaining guys if it would be a repeat of the scenario with Sean.

With all the romantic drama I was enduring, I wasn't sure I could handle an added layer of familial drama. When Nate knocked on the door of my hotel room, I took a steadying breath before opening it. We sat down and he said, "You were mad after I met Sean. You're mad right now."

I shifted awkwardly in my chair. There was something different about talking to Nate in front of the cameras. I saw him through the prism of my childhood, and it was hard to have a conversation without our past refracting through it.

"Last time was hard for me because I wasn't expecting you to screw it up for me," I said. I laughed nervously because I wasn't used to communicating so frankly with my brother. It was easier to hide my vulnerability behind a laugh.

"It was meant to work out that way," Nate said shortly. "How are things going with the guys you've met so far?"

"There's four left."

"Any favorites to win?"

"It isn't winning," I said. Reducing my relationships to a metric of winning and losing revolted me. Each of the last four guys were real people with feelings and emotions as deep as mine. This wasn't *The Amazing Race*. Actual lives were being woven together, and in the end two would intertwine far beyond the show.

"It is winning," Nate insisted. "It's winning you. Who stands out?"

"Who stands out?" I echoed him, suddenly defensive of my last four guys. I didn't want to verbally trot them out to him so he could judge them.

"You're just going to say they really are all great. Blah, blah, blah."

Nate's skepticism was as strong as ever, and I wilted a little inside.

• • •

A few weeks later, it was time for my family to meet Chris. They were flown out to Antigua, and a meeting was set up in a historic château. I wasn't worried about my parents. I was excited to tell them Chris was the one, and I knew they would be able to see what a good and decent person he was. But I was worried about Nate's reaction, and even though I didn't fully understand why, I wanted his validation. The situation felt similar to when I was a girl and tried to play football to impress him and win his approval. It hadn't worked then, and I'd been left with bruises, both on the inside and outside.

I wasn't the only nervous one to talk with my brother, though. For his predate interview, Chris shared that he hoped Nate wouldn't make a snap judgment of him. You only get one chance for a first impression, and he wanted to make sure my family knew he had fallen for me. I knew he was a keeper.

. . .

I met Chris outside the château's lobby so we could walk in together. He came up holding a brilliantly-hued bouquet of tropical flowers for my mom. I met his gaze and instantly knew that no matter what Nate said, Chris would be able to handle it. I put my arms around his neck and tightly embraced him. Hand in hand, we went inside.

Chris gave my mom a hug and the flowers and shook hands with my dad and brother. We sat down to chat before dinner. My dad spoke first and asked with a gentle smile, "Why should Desiree choose you?"

"I think I was fortunate enough to find the one," Chris responded without hesitation, and despite my nerves, I was filled with warmth. He fearlessly said I was the one, even though I hadn't been able to say the same to him. It filled me with happiness.

Nate took over, and I was instantly on edge again. He asked, "What were your first impressions of her?"

"She's beautiful," Chris said easily. "I first thought that she's very attractive, and I wanted us to see what else could be there."

As I listened to Chris, Nate's hold on me slipped away because I realized I had all the security and love I could ever need. Both were embodied in the man who sat next to me, answering Nate's rapid-fire questions with ease.

"Was there a point when you thought that this girl isn't into me because she has a stronger connection with someone else?" Nate pressed.

"When you find the girl you're interested in, whether you meet her in your hometown or elsewhere, you pursue her," Chris responded. "You ask her out on a date, but at the same time there might be other people doing the same thing—you just don't get to see those other people doing it. But in this case, you do see it. I'm confident in what we've had and what we have so far. I don't care what else is going on because I think what we have is stronger than what someone else has."

His answer was equal parts rational and passionate. I was already in love with him, but his response, along with the next two, made me fall even more.

"Are you confident Des will choose you?"

"Yes."

"Getting engaged and married to her . . . that's what you want?"

"One hundred percent."

• • •

Overall, the day went well. My parents didn't say much, but I wasn't surprised. They weren't used to the perpetual presence of the cameras and couldn't fully relax. However, my dad told me he trusted my decisions, and my mom genuinely liked Chris. I was fairly certain that Chris, when he and my dad had gone off alone, had asked for my hand in marriage and that my dad had said yes. I should've been elated, considering how good Chris and my parents were getting along, but I kept waiting for Nate to say something contrarian. As the day progressed, the knots in my shoulders tightened every time he said anything.

Soon it was time for Chris to leave. I kissed him goodbye, wishing I could linger in his arms forever but comforted that I would see him again soon. Then I went inside to talk with Nate on the porch. We settled into chairs and faced each other. Over the course of the evening, I hadn't been able to tell what he was thinking. Even now, reading him was impossible, so I didn't know what he would say. He looked at me evenly and said, "If you choose him, I think you are making the right choice."

I could hardly believe my ears. No matter what he had said, I would've continued on with Chris, but having his validation was an unexpected blessing.

"That's nice to hear," I said.

"Just see where it goes," he added.

I hesitated, wary again, and asked, "Any concerns you have?"

"Yeah," he said. "There are a couple of things we should probably talk about."

"Okay," I responded, internally clamming up yet trying to stay calm. He kept going.

"For instance, when we were back in Los Angeles, there were still a couple guys that were left, and I could tell that you really cared about Brooks. But now that ship has sailed, so to speak. Were you disappointed in any way? Are you hurt in any way?"

Brooks was the last person I wanted to discuss, and Nate was the last person I wanted to discuss him with. But it was a fair question, and it was also a question I knew a lot of people would have.

"To be honest," I said, "I was really hurt. I was hurt because it was a surprise. I didn't know what to feel, and I was hurt because I did put a lot into my relationship with Brooks. I did fall for him. And then after he left, it took me a long time to finally get over that."

"You realized you couldn't change him," Nate said.

"I don't know," I answered, deflated. I wasn't sure where the conversation was headed, but Nate surprised me. He said, "If you choose to accept Chris, I trust your decision."

I smiled. Genuinely smiled. "I'm glad you're here," I said. "I'm glad you like Chris."

And it was true.

. . .

I was finally able to pinpoint the confusing state of my thoughts surrounding Nate. I knew I was on the right track with Chris, and nothing would deter me from that. But Nate, aside from our differences, was an outside and skeptical perspective on the confusing world I'd been living in for the past few months. He was cynical about reality TV and unmoved by what anyone else might think of him. As much as I didn't like to admit it, he had been right about Sean and me—we didn't end up together and he'd said so right away. Hearing that he thought Chris was right for me was reassuring because he, of all people, would call things exactly as he saw them.

At the end of the day, I realized how happy I was that things had worked out the way they had. Almost every other star of *The Bachelor* or *The Bachelorette* still has two contenders at that point, and both of them meet their family. My mom, dad, and Nate met only Chris, and it was so nice that they were able to focus on him without the confusion of knowing another guy was coming the very next day. They didn't have to worry about forming quick opinions, and my dad didn't have to give two men permission to ask for my hand in marriage. And as I considered the week ahead, I was thrilled that I would have so much time to spend with Chris. My heart was no longer divided, and I could pour all my attention and effort into us.

Many people thought I did *The Bachelorette* all wrong by moving on and narrowing down to Chris so quickly. But I got to spend tons of one-on-one time with the guy I chose before we got engaged, which was a huge blessing, and I would never change it.

FOURTEEN

PROPOSAL . . . TAKE TWO!

It looked like Desiree Hartsock's dream of falling
in love had turned into a nightmare. But things
took yet another surprising turn on Monday.

—US WEEKLY

A storm was brewing.

You could see it in the form of dark clouds sweeping their way across the preternatural blue Antigua sky and diluting it to gray. I stared up at them and willed them to go away. Today was it. The final day in this arduous journey that had taken me around the world and through twenty-five relationships and twenty-four breakups. I had my fingers, eyes, and legs crossed that there wouldn't be any more!

Today was the day Chris would propose . . . I hoped. My

stomach was in knots, and I silently repeated the speech I would recite before he got down on one knee. I had zero doubts in my mind. I loved Chris. But before he proposed, I needed to tell him what happened with Brooks. I couldn't get engaged without full disclosure, and I prayed he would understand that while I'd gotten off track, he was and had always been the one for me.

"The weather is looking bad," one of the producers said as we got into the limo to drive to the proposal site. I could hardly believe it. Here I was, heart pounding, dressed in a formal gown with my hair and makeup done to the nth degree, adorned in jewelry, mic'd up, and with the end of this roller coaster of a ride finally in sight . . . only to be told we might have to turn around.

I'd had a rough time getting ready to film that morning and had to do shot after shot of B-roll. I'd stand on my balcony, cupping a mug of tea or writing in my journal, trying to look contemplative and serene. Occasionally I would scan the horizon. It was hard because I was so antsy. I was finally to the finish line, and after the emotional tumult I'd been through, I wanted to be done with filming and in the arms of the man I loved.

By the time we pulled up to the proposal site, rain was battering away at the roof of the car and running down the windows in rivulets.

"We're going into holding," the producer told me from the front seat of the car. That meant we would stay where we were, ready to go, until the rain subsided. I kept going over my speech, trying to prepare for the big moment. But then a bright white spike of lightning split the sky, followed almost immediately by a rumble of thunder.

"I'm sorry to say this, but we have to wait until tomorrow," the producer told me gently, knowing how much I wanted to see Chris. "It's too dangerous."

The proposal site was on top of an oceanside hill, which made it a prime target for lightning.

I nodded and swallowed down the words I so desperately wanted to say to Chris. I tried to see through the rain out the window. I knew Chris was nearby. It was agonizing to know he was so close yet I couldn't see him.

We drove slowly because of the torrent, and my car crawled its way back to my bungalow. Seeing its familiar shingled roof was almost cruel. When I'd left, I'd desperately hoped I'd be returning engaged to the love of my life. But here I was, back where I started, no Chris by my side.

I went in and changed out of my proposal gown into a T-shirt and lounge shorts. I discarded my heels by the dress, slipped off my earrings, and spent a good fifteen minutes scrubbing the ten pounds of mascara, foundation, and eyeliner off my face. In the quiet of the bungalow and still enveloped in the disappointment of the day, I was tempted to fall into my habitual patterns of thinking—to tell myself Chris wouldn't be able to accept me and that my greatest fear, that I was unlovable, was true. But I stopped myself and took a good look at how far I'd come. I knew how God loved me through every twist and turn and saw me worthy of so much, even after I had trusted my own desires. It hit me that I was deserving of the gift of love through Chris. I prayed, giving my anxieties over to God. No matter what happened tomorrow, I refocused on the truth: I knew what it was to be loved by God and, because of that, I could love someone for the right reasons. Okay, stop the eye rolls! I know that phrase has been a *tad* overused on the show, but it was one hundred percent true. I no longer needed relationships to be validated or feel worthy. I looked in the bathroom mirror and truly saw myself. Me. Without the fancy gowns, thick makeup, and discreetly placed mic. Before, I'd let others define how I felt and acted, but with my heart reset, I knew God accepted me just as I was and, most powerfully, that he always had. God's grace washed over me, and I felt more peace in that short moment than I had in my entire journey as the Bachelorette. I felt a convergence of all the roads that had led me here and all the relationships that had guided my steps down them, enabling me to choose freedom in Christ over the lies of the enemy.

I knew no matter what happened at the proposal tomorrow, I was ready. I could only hope, with every bit of my being, that Chris would be ready too when he heard what I had to say.

. . .

The next day, the producers took even more B-roll of me staring off the balcony of my bungalow and then getting ready, once again, for the proposal.

I got into the same dress as before. It was a nude, one-shoulder Randi Rahm gown with a beaded appliqué running down one side. It transformed me as much as any Cinderella dress ever could. My hair was styled once again into the same elegant updo, and I slipped on the same heels and earrings. It was like *The Proposal* meets *Groundhog Day*. I was dressed up and ready to either step into the fairy tale I always wanted but never thought I deserved until these past weeks . . . or leave completely heartbroken. Whatever happened, I knew God would be with me.

I had another moment for reflection when I was interviewed

for the last time before the proposal. Sitting there on the cusp of the unknown, dying to see Chris yet terrified about what he would think after I told him everything, I said, "Never did I think I would be this girl in a beautiful gown with a handsome prince. I've always stayed hopeful about meeting someone who would love me as much as I love them." It hit me then just how far I'd come and that my aching, empty heart had finally found peace. Raw emotions came over me, and my eyes filled with tears. I struggled to stay composed. Looking straight into the camera, I spoke from my heart. "It's hard for me to accept how much Chris loves me because I've never felt that before. Not only do I want to give my heart to someone, they want to give it to me."

Regardless of what awaited me that day, I, the girl who used to hide in closets to hide her hurts, told the world about my deepest hope and most vulnerable desire that I'd carried my whole life and, even with an uncertain future, stood in my truth.

• • •

Once the interview was over, the only thing to do was to go get my man—if he would have me. We arrived at the proposal site once again. The show had arranged for a wood deck to be erected atop the grassy hill, adorned with tropical plants in big urns and rustic barrels. It was the sort of setting that anyone would want to get engaged in, but I barely registered the artfully constructed ambience. All I wanted was to see Chris and share my heart with him. Minutes ticked by, and I kept scanning the path leading to the deck, dying for him to appear. Nervously, I rocked back and forth on my heels.

Finally, he rounded the corner. My first thought was that

he looked *good*. He wore a perfectly tailored black suit with a coordinating black skinny tie, and he walked confidently up the path that cut through the grass and led to where I waited on the deck.

As he got closer, though, I could see his face was pinched with nerves. Little did I know that he'd gotten only five hours of sleep and woken up early to have some time alone on the beach. He'd sat on the sand and thought about the big moment and wondered if I was in the same place as he was. For all he knew, Drew was still in the picture and also preparing to propose. He already knew Brooks had left, but it was impossible for him to know I'd sent Drew home and that he was the only guy who had met my family.

I smiled at him, trying to give him reassurance, though I'd been firmly instructed not to say anything until he started talking.

With a deep breath, Chris stepped onto the platform. The platform trembled slightly beneath me, and I realized that Chris was so nervous that his leg was shaking. When he spoke, his voice was low. I had to lean in to hear. He said, "We're here."

"We're here," I said back, holding tightly to his hands, drawing strength from his presence.

"I couldn't be more happy to have had this journey with you," he continued. "I'm really happy we got to create all those memories. I love that time we had in Germany where we danced. I fell in love with you there."

He began to drop to one knee, but I couldn't let the proposal happen without telling him everything. Impulsively, I reached out to stop him and said, "Can I say a few things?"

"Don't say—" he cut himself off and pulled away from me,

disbelief reeling across his face because the poor guy thought I was about to break up with him. "Okay . . . okay . . ."

There was no going back. I held tightly to his hands and stared up into his face.

"I said goodbye to Drew earlier this week, and you're the only one here. And you're the only one who met my family," I told him. I wavered for a moment. I knew I had to keep going, even though this next part was the hardest. "I was torn apart by Brooks leaving. I loved him, and throughout the journey, I was torn between the two of you. I feel like . . ." my voice broke, and the tears I'd struggled so hard to hold back sprang to my eyes. Chris looked hard at me, still unsure about what I was saying. "I hate it, but I feel like I was so blinded by my feelings for Brooks that I couldn't see the one thing I always needed was always in front of me. You've been by my side from the very beginning. You never lost sight of what we could be, and for that I am so grateful. I thank you every day for never giving up. And you mean the absolute world to me. Chris, I love you. I love you so much."

At that, Chris's face lit up like the bright, unabashed sunshine that had broken across the rainy Antigua morning. Relief, love, and pure happiness filled his eyes.

"Do you want to grow old together?" Chris asked. "Do you want to share your experiences with me? Can I share mine with you?" Just as he had that first night we met, he went down on one knee. Only this time it wasn't to tie a shoe. This time he was asking me to be his wife. "Desiree Eileen Hartsock, I want to be your first, and I want to be your last." He pulled out a black ring box and opened it. Sunlight caught the stunner inside, but I barely saw it. I only had eyes for him. "Will you marry me?"

"Yes," I said. "A thousand times yes."

I hadn't planned that response, which is featured in my favorite movie, *Pride & Prejudice*, but I meant every word. If it worked for Jane Bennet, it could definitely work for me!

The rest of that day went by in a flash. I could tell him I loved him over and over again. I could hold his hand and kiss him when I pleased. The doubts, stresses, and fears that had plagued me since the first night of filming were gone.

We went back to the bungalow for dinner and champagne and simply soaked up the just-engaged exhilaration. Like every other engaged woman, I finally got to actually look at my ring, and I was blown away. It was a four-carat, cushion-cut diamond, and it sat among two hundred other tiny diamonds dotting an intertwining rose gold and platinum band. I loved Chris's reasoning for choosing this specific ring. The intertwining rose gold and platinum represented me and him as our lives wove together and reached the top of the diamond. Chris had no way of knowing this, but I'd wanted a rose gold ring! Simply put—he did good. *Real good.* Every time the ring caught my eye, I couldn't believe it was mine. My entire life, I had admired hundreds of rings on other brides' hands, never thinking I'd ever have one on my own. Now I had an exquisite diamond sparkler given to me by my one true love. Of course, I would've said yes to a ring made of brass. Heck, I would've said yes to a piece of twine. Never in a million years did I ever think I'd be sitting in the Caribbean, engaged not only to someone I'd met on a TV show but to a beautiful man who loved me fiercely and openly. And this ring truly symbolized the new beginning in my life and the faithfulness of God.

Hard times lay ahead of us. I think we both were aware. The show hadn't even aired, and online rumors were already spawning fast and furiously about what had happened with Brooks. Chris and I would be tested beyond our wildest beliefs once the show's season released and social media began to attack us.

But for that beautiful day, we were two people who were madly in love, and nothing could touch us.

FIFTEEN

PAPS, TROLLS, AND FLACKS

So who did Desiree choose to give her heart to in the end?

—*El ONLINE*

Life after *The Bachelorette* should've been happily ever after. Like a modern-day princess, I had a diamond-laden engagement ring on my finger and would soon be moving to a waterfront property in Seattle. In comparison to the tiny studio apartment I was leaving behind, it would be a veritable palace. With the financial opportunities that resulted from the show, my money woes that had haunted me since childhood were gone, and for the first time ever, I would have a definable place to call home. But things were anything but storybook happy.

Chris and I couldn't be public about our relationship because viewers couldn't know how the show ended. While I waited to be reunited with Chris, I lived alone in my shoebox apartment in Santa Monica. I was only a block from the beach and quickly fell into a routine of waking up, grabbing a coffee, and strolling along the boardwalk. With only the soundtrack of gulls, waves, and wind in my ears, I found peace in solitude. But the peace-giving solitude was an illusion. Photos of me appeared in tabloids and online, photos that I had no idea were being taken and sold to entertainment outlets by the paparazzi. I was used to fans approaching me for hugs and selfies, but I wasn't prepared for the long-distance lenses of paparazzi cameras, which would capture me doing the most mundane things, like shopping at T.J. Maxx or reading a book at the beach. I never saw the photographers and never knew when the photos were taken. It was disturbing to know that someone was not only watching me but documenting my actions so they could profit from them. I felt violated and scared, not to mention constantly paranoid. I became isolated, choosing to stay in the confines of my apartment because every time I went out, I didn't know if photographers were watching and following me. As a young woman alone in the city, being followed was a terrifying experience.

During this time, I had to watch the episodes of *The Bachelorette* a week before they aired so I could blog about them. I would give Chris a breakdown of each episode so there wouldn't be any surprises when he watched the show with the rest of the world later in the week. To his credit, he was my rock during that chaotic time and never made me feel bad about any of my decisions. I, though, felt trapped in a time warp, stuck in the past and unable to freely rest in the present. All week long, I relived events I'd long since put behind me, and I couldn't vent to friends because the results of the show were strictly confidential. It was just me and my guys—Ben & Jerry's and occasionally "Two-Buck Chuck." I began to write a daily devotional for young women as an escape from my internal stress. While I typed out the lessons I'd learned, I think deep down I was trying to keep my own spirits hopeful.

My only respite came every ten days. We would meet up at a vacation home rental and hang out for the entire weekend. Amid the isolation, paranoia, and stress from the show airing, these weekends became the brightest moments of my life. We couldn't go anywhere, but it didn't matter. Alternating between candid conversations and comfortable silences, we basked in the sunshine, dipped our feet in whatever pool was in the backyard of the rental, and soaked up each other's company—blissfully never turning on the TV or checking our phones.

It seemed like I would blink and the weekend would be over. Then we would have to separate and head back into the real world. And the real world got darker and more suffocating by the moment.

My first glimpse into just how intense things would get came when episode six aired, when I had sent Juan Pablo home. I didn't think too much about it because I thought it was clear that we weren't a fit and assumed the viewers understood. I'd given the relationship a fair chance, and though he was like my own personal David Beckham with his gorgeous looks and soccer skills, there wasn't enough to build a relationship on. But when he was eliminated, the internet went wild. Thousands of notifications popped up on my phone as my social media was inundated with people telling me how stupid and awful I was for letting him go. The uproar seemed like it would never stop. Over and over again, those hurtful words flashed in front of my eyes as I desperately tried to delete the notifications. It's hard to explain what it's like to experience such a tide of rage. "You're an idiot!" scrolled across my Twitter screen, I kid you not, about five hundred times, if not more. I was simultaneously shocked and bewildered. After all, there are things to be genuinely angry about in this world. Things like poverty and injustice. From the vitriolic reactions, you'd think I murdered Juan Pablo and his whole family, not simply eliminated him from a dating show.

Things got much worse once the last few episodes aired, the ones where Brooks left and I moved on with Chris. Looking back, I think certain factors were partially to blame. A famous TV blogger who posts spoilers about shows predicted early on that Brooks would leave the show and then come back at the finale to win me back. Well, he got one part right. Brooks indeed left the show. *Buuut* he never came back. Tons of viewers read those spoilers and assumed they were facts. So when they watched the episodes, they mentally eliminated all the other guys I was dating and only followed the story line occurring between Brooks and me. By the time they realized we didn't end up together, they'd become emotionally invested in our relationship and couldn't conceive of me being with anyone else.

The verbiage and answers I took on to keep the ending a secret may not have helped my situation either. I thought I was doing a favor by making the ending a surprise, but in reality my downplay of finding love and being engaged did just the opposite. This overall demeanor only played into everyone's assumptions about how things would go and made it harder for them to accept an alternate ending. If I could go back, I would stand up for myself because, at the end of the day, it was my story and my life.

All the while, I couldn't share my true feelings with anyone because the show's finale was considered akin to a state secret. All the confidentiality isolated me even more, fueling my feelings of anxiety and depression. My name and face were everywhere, and everyone was talking about me—yet I'd never been so alone.

Engagement should be such a happy time, yet mine was clouded with judgmental and outright cruel comments. They settled around me like a fog that only got thicker with each new episode. I was completely in love and also completely drained. Chris was my only light through the mind-numbing haze. He'd gone back to his daily work life, and just as he was during filming, he remained steadfast through it all.

I, though, had more time to be distracted by it. I sat in my studio, reading terrible things about myself, watching the episodes as they aired. Even past leads and contestants criticized me, which was the last thing I expected. They were some of the few people who knew what it was like to be in my shoes, so their judgment hurt even more. Feeling my way through the gloom was hard. I tried to give everything to God, but cruelty from other people, no matter how thick your skin is, is damaging. When the brokenness of the world envelops you so completely, you realize just how much all of us need salvation and why—it's impossible for us as individuals to handle the darkness of humanity. Only through God and his grace can we find a way forward.

When the finale aired, I was ecstatic. Finally, Chris and I were free to be public and I could put the negativity in the past and focus on the future. My next step was to move to Seattle. Chris and I had to do a last batch of publicity work in New York, where we had to defend our relationship again and again. But once that was finished, he came back to California with me and we rented a van to pack up my stuff. I couldn't load up those boxes fast enough.

For the first time in ages, my spirits lifted as we hit the road and headed toward home and a fresh start.

SIXTEEN

THE HONEYMOON IS OVER

Ninth Bachelorette Desiree Hartsock, a fan
favorite, has been thriving both personally and
professionally since her season ended in 2013.

—*SCREEN RANT*

A new fiancé.
    A new home.
A new job.
A brand-new life.

As Chris and I embarked on our journey from California to
Seattle with my entire life packed into our rented van, I was on
cloud nine.

Chris gave me a newfound happiness. His strength and

consistency got me through the struggle of watching the show air, and I relied on his steadfastness.

Accustomed to moving, I was exhilarated to head to Seattle to begin a brand-new life with Chris. I had never been north of Napa Valley but was eager to see what awaited us in the land of highbrow coffee and rain. We sang at the top of our lungs to every single road trip song all the way from California to Washington. I remember the moment I saw my new home. I was struck silent in awe at the sight of the Seattle skyline emerging ahead of us. A cluster of skyscrapers sparkled in the morning light against a rim of mountains while a beautiful body of water nestled between the two. The grandness beckoned us to come and be a part of this thriving city.

I'm home, I thought as a huge grin split across my face, and I tightened my grip on Chris's free hand.

• • •

My hopes for Seattle and my experience of it were the equivalent of an Instagram-versus-reality post: my hopes were high, but the reality was an earth-to-Des disappointment. I loved the natural beauty of the hilly and rainy city. But aside from contending with a perpetually gloomy and gray forecast (which often felt quite atmospheric), I had a lot of hurt that I needed to process before I could truly feel peace about my life in a new city.

Try as I would to ignore, block, or put a happy face on the ugly, insulting, and negative comments I received after the show's finale, I was deeply wounded. I thought I would feel secure with Chris by my side and the paparazzi left back in California. But the attention we received from strangers put me back in the antsy and stressed mindset I'd had in Cali. Anywhere we went, from the grocery store to a fast-food restaurant, eyes watched me, and I would catch people holding up their phones to "secretly" film us. Even when fans approached us for hugs or to take photos, I was always on guard, steeling myself in case they had something negative to say. I am grateful for kind fans and people who offered well wishes. But during that time, with the laser focus on us after the show, I was on high alert and anxious about my every move being judged. Eventually, I opted to stay home and go out less to avoid the whispers, stares, and incognito photos.

But I couldn't always hide. For example, Chris and I were scheduled to ride on a *Bachelor/Bachelorette*-themed float for the famous Rose Bowl Parade in Los Angeles. We boarded the rose-festooned float along with Bachelor Nation alums Jason and Molly Mesnick and the newly announced Bachelor, Chris Soules. The float began its leisurely journey down the street, and we waved to the crowds who watched and cheered from the bleachers. Suddenly, a man pointed to us and yelled out, "She doesn't love you, Chris!"

Here we were—engaged (at that point, our wedding was less than a month away)—and a random stranger was publicly decrying our relationship. Even after we wed, we continued to receive hurtful comments that diminished our marriage and questioned my intentions.

I'm such a different person now that it seems silly to even write this since attention is something I should have expected going onto *The Bachelorette*. The truth is that I thought my journey would go smoothly. I assumed I would make all the right decisions and be loved as America's sweetheart. A bit naive? Definitely. But I was a normal girl thrust into a bright and unforgiving spotlight and had no idea how much the opinions of others would affect me and shape my view of myself.

The more our relationship was questioned, the more I tried to defend it. I never felt the need to retaliate, but I wanted to be understood and I wanted our relationship to be seen the way we saw it: as an honest, real, and true love.

Aside from those stresses, I was also figuring out how my dreams fit into my new life. There is a preconceived notion that as the Bachelorette, you become a millionaire and are set for the rest of your life and can pursue whatever goals you have. In reality, you're paid pennies compared with what an actor or even a stand-in actor would receive on a scripted TV show. Also, you don't receive any royalties. So as the show aired a year later in Australia, and then again in the UK, and everywhere else across the world, I received new waves of mixed comments—and not a dime to show for it. Granted, money isn't the reason I went on the show. I would've taken any dollar amount and considered myself lucky. For me, the payment as the Bachelorette was a bailout to settle past-due bills, chip away at my student loans, and help me stay afloat for the three months after the show when I couldn't work because of the media obligations.

My season aired in 2013, right when Instagram was picking up. Over the next few years, social media marketing became a thing and influencers appeared on this new digital frontier. To say I was prime influencer material would be a laughable statement. My experience with taking photos was limited to the low-quality photos I would capture with my awesome, dinosaur-era flip phone or the many disposable cameras I loved to take everywhere I went. But I was immediately seen as an influencer because of my social media following and title as the former Bachelorette.

The role didn't come naturally to me, but I played it because the partnerships funded my business ventures. To this day, I'm so thankful to all the businesses and companies I've worked with in the past on social media collaborations. Little did they know, they were the reason I was able to become a designer.

In this new reality, we both worked long days, which left us exhausted and moody. We also discovered huge differences in our communication or, as you probably have gathered from the previous chapters, my lack of communication.

Chris comes from a family of over-sharers, and it's one of the most beautiful and abundant ways of communicating. No topic is off limits. I love having multiple confidants with whom to share my worries, joys, and life. I am so lucky to have each one of his family members as my own. But in the beginning, Chris's communication style clashed with mine, and this fueled many of our frustrations during our first year together.

Our disagreements rose from mindless bickering over such silly things as driving directions or who was right in a banal conversation. We quickly learned that stubbornness is something we both have in spades and that my past habits of running from conflict were carrying over into our relationship.

When it came to quarrels, Chris would want to hash out what was said, what was actually meant, and figure out how to resolve the argument. Me? Well, I would go mute. A flood of tears would fill my eyes, and I would walk away. It was an auto response, programmed over a lifetime. I am the type of person who needs to take a night to reflect on the argument. I had never felt confident in articulating my feelings verbally and needed time to figure out exactly what my feelings were before I could talk to Chris again.

My old communication pattern wasn't ideal and was

something I had to consistently work on. I will say, seven years later, that I can stay in a conversation even if it's hard. I've even come to appreciate the challenge of overcoming certain triggers. Growing pains in a relationship aren't so bad when you're able to see where each person may need some watering and growth. And when it's you, you get the chance to rise above old demons, with someone you love at your side.

Pride was another issue I didn't realize I had. Every time Chris offered constructive criticism, I found myself fighting against my pride to accept what he was saying. It makes sense why criticism would hurt me—negative words have left their mark on me since childhood, so I couldn't recognize criticism as a good thing and would become defensive. Chris and his family can hear criticism from each other in a positive way because they are accustomed to it and know it comes from a place of love. Initially, Chris couldn't understand why I didn't want his "help."

"Babe, you really should look into this for your business and maybe talk with this person to see where you need help," Chris would mention coyly.

"I know what I'm doing," I would say sharply. My independent streak was strong and had been ever since I was a child. I taught myself how to French braid my own hair when I was just five years old. And I would take things apart just to know how to put them back together. Since I fought hard to provide for myself before this relationship, I didn't want to be told what to do or how to do things, especially in regard to my professional dreams. I will be the first to admit that this trait is not the most helpful for any entrepreneur. Thank the Lord that through years of prayer and fighting through the lump in my throat as I listen to Chris offer advice, I no longer allow pride to get in the way of what have always been heartfelt suggestions. Now I actively seek advice and have benefited immensely from the guidance of others, including Chris.

I've learned that it's easy to let our past show up in our present. The ways we treat others and how we treat ourselves stem from our perceptions of what has been done to us and how we have internalized those events. We can overcome these ingrained hurts or let them define us and mold our reactions.

I'm grateful for the way God has used my marriage to help me grow. It can be hard because relationships involve two people becoming one. But that's also its strength and purpose. We are a single unit, but within our marriage we are able to develop individually while having someone to rely on and grow with. I think that's the key to a happy marriage: love and the willingness to strive together—to be committed to working on oneself while also helping your partner become who God intended them to be.

Chris and I will never be perfect, but we will always be in love, and we will always be striving together. For me, that's true love. Receiving and giving it has been the greatest joy of my life.

SEVENTEEN

WEDDING BLISS (AND A FEW WEDDING WOES)

"Bachelorette Desiree Hartsock and Chris Siegfried
Look Madly in Love on Their Wedding Day."

—*A HEADLINE FROM E! ONLINE*

Weddings are a lot like reality television. There are the stars (bride and groom, of course), hair and makeup crews, cameras, and wedding planners, who are basically producers but without the comfortable walking shoes and headset. Combine those factors with my many years of bridal industry experience, and I should've been a wedding pro.

As it turns out, just like any other bride, I dealt with a lot of stress. But there was a key difference. Most brides only have to worry about wedding colors and where to seat their weird uncle. The network was interested in possibly televising the event. Chris and I were open to the possibility. America had seen our entire love story, so it only made sense to share this final, culminating chapter as well. Talks ensued—and then kept ensuing as we tried to figure out what a televised wedding would look like and what the network's vision might be for it. Months passed, and there was no definitive answer about when our wedding might occur. At one point, the production company suggested holding the wedding at the Bachelor mansion. I was reticent. Those grounds held many memories, both good and bad. It would be special for the viewers but didn't feel intimate or right for us.

Finally, six months had come and gone and we were done waiting.

"Let's just pick a date and go for it," I told Chris one day. The minute he agreed, I was relieved. We picked January 18, 2015, as our wedding date. Once the date was decided, we jumped right into planning mode because we had only six months and needed to figure everything out. Like, *everything.* The only other confirmed detail we had was, well, that we would get married.

Some decisions came easily. Since we were living in Seattle but it wasn't either of our hometowns, we decided to have the wedding in California. Back in my bridal stylist days, I'd worked at salons in Beverly Hills and Costa Mesa and had heard about a beautiful glass chapel located atop the rocky cliffs near Palos Verdes that run parallel to the ocean. I was intrigued by this notion of a glass chapel, where you could have the architectural beauty of a church yet still be immersed in nature. The minute we stepped inside its glass walls, we booked it. A library was located nearby in Redondo Beach, and taken by its historic nature and quaint literary vibe, we decided to host the reception there. I could already see it: a breezy, elegant ceremony followed by a vintage-inspired reception full of fresh blooms and old books.

Other decisions were tricky, particularly the dress. Or in my case, two dresses—a ceremony gown and a reception dress—because who doesn't want a wardrobe change? Since bridal is my factory default setting, you'd think I'd have known exactly what I wanted for my wedding day outfits. But it turns out that years of seeing every bridal dress iteration possible makes things confusing when you can suddenly pick only two.

At the time, I was designing an eponymous collection with Maggie Sottero, a renowned wedding gown label. They would create both my dresses once I showed them my vision. I started with the tour de force, the ceremony gown. I sat down with my sketch pad and thought about features I hadn't seen a lot of. I sketched a one-shoulder gown with an illusion back and ivory lace appliqués over a blush lining. It was soft, romantic, and natural. And the only sparkle came in the form of subtle beads reflecting against the light because I'd worn quite enough sparkles on the shows and was tired of feeling like a bedazzled disco ball.

For the reception dress, I was inspired by dresses from the 1920s . . . and my desire to wear something that felt unconstricting and wouldn't require bathroom assistance so I could effectively drop it like it's hot, should the need arise. I sketched out a slinky silhouette with vintage-inspired beading reminiscent of a *Great Gatsby* party dress. Pleased, I sent the sketches off for manufacturing. Both gowns turned out exactly as I had envisioned them. When I slipped into the ceremony dress for the first time, I felt at ease and like myself.

When you're planning your wedding with your partner,

you're both sorting through an overwhelming number of options and making decision after decision. Some of them are big, like whether you should add five thousand dollars to your budget. Others are small, like whether the napkins should be eggshell or ivory. No matter their importance, they add up and can quickly lead to option fatigue. In theory, planning a wedding is quite romantic. But when you've spent hours at your coffee table with sticky notes and a seating chart illustration and you find yourself debating with your partner over whether your old college friend should sit closer to the dance floor than his coworker, you realize it isn't as glamorous as it might seem. Even the strongest couples can fall victim to the wedding planning blues.

We had the added dimension of collaborations and press. We needed to choose which publications would run our wedding photos. Several wedding industry professionals offered their services, and we needed to review their pitches and see who truly understood our style. So we had a *lot* to navigate, and there wasn't a single wedding planning blog with an article on how to decide which magazine should get rights to your photos.

Wedding planning was taking over our lives, and we needed to reclaim our normalcy. Otherwise, we might've found ourselves headed to marriage therapy before we were even married! So we learned to compartmentalize. We decided that we would discuss wedding planning, especially the finances and costs of everything (because it gave me anxiety), from five to six o'clock each night—then open a bottle of wine and enjoy each other's company. Once we implemented this strategy, the process was a lot more manageable and fun, as it should be.

Before I knew it, our wedding was just a few days away. Everything was going smoothly, which naturally meant something was about to go wrong. My parents flew in from Ohio, and I went to meet them at their hotel. I wanted to welcome them and also check out their outfits. Since they don't dress up often, I wanted them to be comfortable and to feel good on the wedding day. My mom's dress was lovely, but the hem was much too long. I can sew, but the hem not only had a scallop, it also had beading on top of that. A quickie hem was out of the question. Thinking fast, I decided we could fix the issue with a higher pair of heels. That day. Because the wedding was in less than forty-eight hours!

Then my dad opened the wardrobe to show me his attire: an elegant suit jacket and shirt hung on the rack . . . but without any pants. Somehow they'd never made it from Ohio to California. Immediately, I got on the phone and called suit places to see if we could get some pants. Palos Verdes, where our venue was located, is remote and sits far above the adjoining cities. This is one of its biggest appeals—except for when you need suit pants ASAP.

I finally found a suit place and another shop where we could look for shoes for my mom. Both parents in tow, I drove down the winding Palos Verdes road, trying to stay calm and reassuring myself that we would find a pair of men's pants and women's heels. Luckily, the suit store had pants for my dad, but they were much too long and pooled around his ankles.

"No problem," I said. "I'll hem them."

Pants in our possession, we headed off to the next shop and found some heels for my mom. They were tall enough to adjust the length of her dress. We got back to their hotel, and I spent the night before my wedding sewing so fast, you'd think I was on an episode of *Project Runway*.

It was stressful, but little things always go wrong at weddings. The incorrect flowers are delivered, or you realize your veil didn't get steamed, or your bridesmaids never learned how to bustle your train. If you're like me, you end up hemming your dad's pants by hand. And we would learn the morning of the wedding, the ring box had gone the way of my dad's pants and never made it to the venue. The important thing is to remember that you're marrying the love of your life. Even if everything goes perfectly, the flowers will eventually wilt and the cake will be eaten. The thing that lasts longer than the wedding day is the love you take into your marriage, and that's built even before a ring is on your finger.

．　．　．

The wedding day itself started off like any other day—waking up, coffee, breakfast . . . oh, and an entourage of bridesmaids and a glam squad, and there also may have been mimosas. I was surrounded by my closest friends, and the morning was peaceful and lighthearted. One thing I didn't anticipate was how joyful I felt. It was quite a moment when I slipped into my wedding gown. After working with hundreds of brides and going through the highs and lows of the shows, it was my turn to be the happy bride and marry my one true love. I picked up my ribbon-tied bouquet, and my joy turned to excitement at the thought of seeing Chris and doing what I'd wanted to do all along: marry the boy and make him mine.

We decided against a first look. Chris had no idea what I was going to wear, and we didn't see each other until I was at the entrance to the aisle, which added to the anticipation. My nerves began to build as my bridesmaids and I headed to the chapel. One by one, my maids headed to the altar, and then it was just me and my dad. I took his arm, and we stepped through the doors.

The minute Chris saw me, his face broke into an adorable grin, and I couldn't wait to get to him. Walking down the aisle, I marveled at how things had changed. While we were on *The Bachelorette*, he was always walking to me to accept my roses. Now I was going to him. Soon we would walk side by side up the aisle, and that's how we would navigate the world from there on out—side by side, hand in hand, partners forever.

Soon we were both at the altar, staring into each other's eyes as we said our vows and made our lifelong commitment to each other. It was a remarkable moment, made even more powerful by the witness of all our loved ones who had come to share our joy. Weddings are truly unique in that they are one of the few times when your nearest and dearest are in one place at one time in order to celebrate your love.

Joining our special day, we also had the producers who helped my story unfold on TV, some *Bachelor* alums, and even a few of the guys from my season, including Michael Garofola, the six-pack (maybe eight?) Zak Waddell, and yes, even the infamous Brooks. Chris had stayed close with these guys. While Brooks being at our wedding may have been shocking for viewers, Brooks was never the one for me, and the moment he left, so did any feelings I thought I had. Inviting him to our wedding solidified the truth that our past doesn't need to define our future, and it was a great reminder of God's goodness through it all.

Blessed is how I would describe our ceremony. (Though, I will add, I tried to say my wedding vows from memory, and while I managed to get them out, I would recommend writing them down in a cute vow book and reading them. The last thing brides should worry about on their wedding day is performance anxiety.)

Immediately after we tied the knot, we took photos and headed to the reception. The library was a vintage dream come true. Rustic wood bookshelves ran along the walls and were the perfect backdrop to the long banquet-style tables. Multiple floral arrangements in ivory and dark pink spread across each table. Stacks of old books in taupe and cream paid homage to the library setting, while linen favor bags of taffy (one of my favorite treats) sat atop each place setting. I wanted to move into the reception venue and never leave.

For our reception, Chris and I wanted to have a fun party with tons of dancing (and no cheesy wedding songs—"The Macarena" was on our firm "do not play" list). Chris arranged a romantic surprise for our first dance. He got Matt White to perform "Love and Affection," which immediately touched my heart. We'd danced to that song in Germany on our first one-on-one date. Back then I'd known something magical was happening between us, and now here we were, swaying to the same song once again as husband and wife.

After our dance, everyone got out of their seats and joined us on the dance floor. The dance moves were out in full force. Some were good, some were bad, and some were in-between—and Chris and I loved them all.

They say your wedding goes by in the blink of an eye and, oh my goodness, does it ever. It was a blur—but the happiest, warmest, loveliest blur you can imagine, the sort you see just as the sun slips over the horizon at sunset and takes your breath away or when your eyes are misty from realizing just how blessed you are. Our wedding was a blur, but one full of images frozen in time, a mental photo album not just of snapshots but also of feelings. I savor images like when I shared a moment with my dad before he walked me down the aisle and gave me away, locked eyes with Chris for the first time that day, held hands with my bridesmaids and sang at the top of our lungs to the songs, and cut the cake with mediocre success. (It turns out it's not so easy to cut and plate a slice of cake while holding the knife with another person. The Food Network will not be calling either of us anytime soon.)

Before we knew it, we were hugging our friends and family goodbye. My hair was falling loose from its waves, and my train was dirty from dragging on the ground. But those things were testaments to how much fun I'd had. We waved goodbye to everyone and headed off on our honeymoon to Hawaii.

My season on *The Bachelorette* was always framed as a fairy tale, but my time on the show felt more like a soap opera. Thanks to God, I truly did get my happily ever after.

EIGHTEEN

AN UNFILTERED MAMA

Desiree revealed more about how she grew up. Her parents have been married for 35 years, but together for 40 years and she insists that despite being poor she was extremely blessed with lots of love from her family.

—OK! HERE IS THE SITUATION

I was twenty-one, visiting my parents in Florida, using their ancient beast of a computer, when I stumbled across a Word document. Leaning toward the screen, I read it. By the time I reached the end, tears coursed down my cheeks.

. . .

My whole life, the photo of my older sister, Erica, had followed us no matter where we went. It was displayed in whatever place we called home, whether propped up on a side table or hanging on the wall as a silent tribute. But I didn't know much beyond the single grainy image of the Bambi-eyed baby in the incubator and the sparse facts that she was my parents' first child and died shortly after birth.

The document I stumbled across contained my parents' testimony and the story of Erica. Sitting at the computer, I read that she was born by emergency cesarean after my mom had a seizure at home and then another one on the way to the hospital. Her eclampsia wasn't detected early enough, and it threw Erica's birth into mayhem. Erica was immediately flown from Wyoming to a children's hospital in Colorado. My mother couldn't travel with her because she was recovering, and when Erica died eight days later, my mom hadn't gotten to hold her once. Warm tears streamed down my face as I tried to fathom the pain my parents must have felt. This revelation explained a lot, and my heart ached for my mom.

• • •

My parents were born and raised in a tiny Pennsylvania town bordering on Amish country. Old ways overlapped into the new, and seeing buggies and horses plodding down the streets was just as common as seeing cars. Their high school had a graduating class of about fifty kids. My dad says he would instantly get goosebumps as he passed by the locker of the brown-haired, golden-eyed girl with the armful of textbooks. They became high school sweethearts, and as soon as they got married after graduating from trade schools, they left their small Pennsylvania town and set off for Indiana.

Movement defines my parents' lives. Since my dad worked in the construction industry, he easily found jobs across the various states that they traveled to, settled in, and would ultimately leave. From what I gather, company relocations and wanderlust inspired their constant movement. Also, I think my mom was searching for home just as much as she was trying to leave her old home behind. Shortly after my parents settled in Indiana, they moved to Wyoming in search of mountains and cowboys (essentially, I think my dad wanted to be John Wayne). It was their second relocation in an endless chain that continued after my brother was born in Indiana and I was born in Wyoming. Aside from being my birthplace, Wyoming is significant because it's where my parents learned they were expecting Erica and the place where she too was born.

Losing a child is traumatizing and heartbreaking. I can never fully know this pain, but I empathize deeply in my soul and understand my mom better through my own journey into motherhood. I can't imagine losing a baby, and I can't imagine not being able to hold that baby before she died. Erica's death darkened the landscape of my mom's life. Sometimes Mom's grief would roll in as dark clouds of depression or, at other times, disconnection from others.

At the same time, my mom carried this sadness in the best way she knew how and let it drive her into the deeper waters of her faith. My mom's dad was a devout Christian man, and he passed his beliefs down to her. It was my mom who inspired my dad to listen to Billy Graham. Dad was compelled by the salvation message and accepted Jesus into his heart, becoming a first-generation Christian. But it was after the loss of Erica that they fully embraced their faith and found miraculous hope.

Because of health complications from Erica's birth, my mom was told she would never have any other children. My parents cried out to God as my mother sought deliverance from grief and depression. A pastor at their church gave them a prophetic word that they would one day have a son. In faith, they set a plate every night at their dining room table for their future boy.

This son, my brother, came soon thereafter, and two years later I was born.

• • •

Growing up, I never saw my parents so much as raise an eyebrow at each other, much less their voices (now that I'm married, I realize what a feat this is!). My dad often came home with flowers for my mom. My mom would (and still does) kiss and hug my dad to make my brother and I cringe. They aren't extremely expressive people, but their devotion to each other was as steady as the earth beneath my feet. It was a guiding light amid the difficult circumstances I navigated as a child, teen, and young adult and created the deepest longing in my life—to one day have a happy marriage and family of my own. Even while my mom couldn't sit still and we wouldn't settle down long before she felt the itch to move a couple of states over, I knew my parents' marriage was secure and that though we wandered, we were always wandering together. Home sweet home, I realized, wasn't a physical place but rather a feeling found only among us four Hartsocks.

. . .

While my parents' relationship was steady ground, the other areas of their lives caused earth-shaking shifts that sent me stumbling. The continual moving meant that climbing out of poverty was almost impossible, especially with my parents' sporadic health afflictions.

When I was eight years old, Dad was rushed to the hospital due to a work injury where his hand was crushed, leaving his thumb hanging on by only a nerve and other fingers severely hurt. Luckily that nerve kept his thumb in place, and doctors were able to stitch it back together. While the company he worked for was gracious, he went weeks without working so he could recover. Then, just a few years later, another incident would set them back again.

One summer we lived in an RV on a campground amid the mountains. I loved it because it felt like a perpetual outdoor adventure. I was playing outside with the other campground kids when I spotted a red-and-white ambulance cutting its way across the park. It stopped outside our RV, and my hands went clammy. My brother and I stood helpless, too far away to get there in time to see what was happening. We never did reach the ambulance before my mom was taken away to the nearest hospital.

She had been battling flu-like symptoms and, determined not to drain the fledgling family coffers, didn't see a doctor until it was too late. An emergency exploratory surgery revealed that her appendix had burst and gangrene had set in. Our financial situation, along with her health, made it impossible for Mom to pursue her dreams of becoming a nurse. No matter what, though, the helpful, nurturing side of her was always present, and it expressed itself in caregiving for the elderly and as an orderly at out-patient nursing facilities. When it came to raising me, my mom and I had our battles, which often dragged on in silence. Most mother-daughter relationships are tested in high school when puberty and hormones hit, and we were no exception. Our relationship tended to be passive-aggressive, with few words exchanged between us—and when they were, those words weren't kind.

Vanity was the sin of all sins, so neither parent ever praised my outward appearance. If I looked in the mirror too long, I was considered vain or I was often "too thin." Being a young woman and a daughter, I triggered much of my mom's own high school years. Without even knowing it, she was repeating the same script her mother had used with her.

As for my dad, he also wasn't effusive with praise, but he was a great encourager and always said I should be an artist. I often brushed off the praise. It wasn't because I didn't believe him or want to hear the artist part, but I've never liked being told what to do. This oppositional nature has come with me into marriage and entrepreneurship, and it's something I continue to work on to this day.

• • •

Amid the challenges they faced, my parents gave me traits I wouldn't trade for anything. My dad is a gentle man, yet his capacity for life is mystifying. He worked grueling sixty-hour work weeks, and some of those stints were in the dark heart of the earth as a coal miner. Not once did I hear him complain, even though the labor was backbreaking and the shifts bled one into another. While we lived in Indiana, he somehow carved out time to attend Bible school through our church and go on a mission trip to China, despite his insane work schedule. His example left a deep impression on me, and I always strive to work hard without complaining.

My mom gave me the gift of seeing the world without boundaries. I have a chronic travel bug and can adapt to almost anywhere because of her free-spirited approach to life.

I've come to a place where I appreciate my upbringing because my parents did their best amid the alternating dark and light that life brought them. Even though they weren't demonstrative about it, I knew they loved me and that they loved each other.

. . .

When I saw two blue lines on a pregnancy test after Chris and I had been married for a year, I took a deep breath. This was my second chance at family life but with the roles recast. Now I was the mama, and it was a huge step because I didn't know anything about babies beyond glancing at the covers of parenting magazines in the dentist's office. I knew I wanted to shower my kiddos with love and give them roots as well as wings, but I hadn't had real-life examples of that. What would mothering without a clear guide be like? You can't find tips on that in *What to Expect When You're Expecting*.

Luckily, Chris and I settled near his family, and for the first time, I was able to see the beauty of rhythm and routine. A younger version of me would become antsy if I ever stayed put for too long. But I found that my world expanded within the four walls of our home and that the best adventures are built with love and commitment. Currently, we have two young boys and my life is full of routine. It has become a song that is all our own. We have family dinners, dance parties, and fort nights. We go for long walks and cuddle on our couch, and sometimes Chris and I get to sneak away for a date in which we talk about the kids way too much but both secretly love it. Of course, as a working mom, I always seem to be looking for a lost Hot Wheels car while sending a work email from my phone. And I worry about screen time and whether my boys are eating enough vegetables. But I consider it a blessing to have such full hands, because it means my heart is equally as full.

Unrealistic motherhood standards, though!

While motherhood has healed wounds from my childhood, I didn't realize there was a different monster to contend with, a monster fueled by mommy-shaming and comparison traps.

It reaches for all of us mamas as we blearily scroll through social media while holding mugs of reheated coffee, wondering who we are now. I definitely went through a loss of identity during the first few months of motherhood with Asher, our first-born. There was insane pressure from the outside world to get my body back (as if I ever lost it!), make my own organic baby food, and turn our playroom into a mini Montessori classroom with visual stimulation for my six-month-old! I was unsure about who I was and where to find my worth. I was fatigued from the workload of a newborn and struggled to accept my new body and new role as a mom. I was worn down and felt ugly. The whole experience brought a tsunami of emotions (and hormones—the fourth trimester is real).

As I adjusted to motherhood and found myself confronted

with images of seemingly perfect mamas and their cherubic, perfect babies, my heart longed for an unfiltered view of motherhood. I wanted one that wasn't just about sharing Pinterest-worthy nurseries or the popular advice in a social media influencer's Instagram post to go up one size in streetwear to accommodate a baby bump (who does that even work for?). I desired a perspective that didn't gloss over the actual experience of pregnancy, delivery, and postpartum recovery, a view that celebrates motherhood while acknowledging its challenges.

With our first son, I shared about my pregnancy experience and birth story but slowly became bolder to share more of the daily challenges as I saw so many other mamas on social media struggling with the same issues as I was. I realized that maybe, just maybe, I could share that perspective I longed for. I posted my birth story (and didn't spare any of the details of my home birth!) and also started to give glimpses into my everyday life as a working, first-time mom. During this season, I turned to Scripture and found encouragement in Esther's story. She was told she was created "for such a time as this" (Esther 4:14), and those words gave me hope. When I embraced the mindset that motherhood is a season of life God placed me in to care for my child and began to trust him to strengthen my body and mind for the job, I shifted my attention away from my personal desires to how I could use this time to help others. He can't use us to better ourselves or others if we don't trust that he is able to give us the strength and wisdom we need.

Once my second son, Zander, was born, I was even more compelled to be raw and honest about my motherhood story and did something I never thought I would be brave enough to do. I snapped a selfie of my four-day postpartum body while wearing sweats and a sports bra. Then I tapped *Share* on my Instagram. Yes, I still looked pregnant, but as I wrote in my caption,

> It is an absolute miracle what our bodies can do to carry and deliver a baby . . . as a society, we need to embrace the beauty of the body during this time and not expect a new mom to just "bounce" back like her body didn't just go through battle. It's feeling beautiful and courageous in our own skin no matter the stretch marks, extra weight, and whatever else is going on. Grace upon grace upon grace . . . for ourselves and each other.

And then I signed off with, "Long story short. You're awesome, your body rocks, and you're beautiful!"

The post went viral and was reshared by several media outlets. But the thing that meant the most to me was receiving comments from other women who saw themselves in my photo and appreciated having their postpartum bodies celebrated for the wondrous feat of bringing a baby into this world. Seeing how much the image resonated encouraged me to keep sharing, and I continue to do so now, whether it's offering a prayer for mamas struggling to get through the day or talking about how Chris and I make time for date night when we have two kids under four.

As an unfiltered mama, I hope to provide encouragement about the intersection of womanhood, motherhood, and entrepreneurship, no matter who you are or where you come from. While dealing with my own challenges balancing it all, I find it's imperative for mothers to unite in real conversations about our experiences. No one is perfect, but by showing up daily, we discover a greater purpose within ourselves. And by sharing, we are creating the village of support we desperately need.

When we have toddlers running around, we can often lose sight of our own inner lights and the sparks that fuel them. We can end up finding our worth solely in how well we are performing our "duties" as a mother and wife. Our focus is on wiping runny noses and scheduling daycare pickups, and our lights can start to dim. But each of us has giftings, and I firmly believe women should be empowered to pursue them. This looks different for each of us, especially when juggling family life, but discovering our identity outside of wake-up time and bedtime is a rebirth of ourselves. Don't get me wrong, some women do have the gifting of caring for babies and children full-time, and we must seek the Lord's guidance on that. I just knew quickly that wasn't the calling on my life, and I needed to pursue what fueled me.

By the time I had Zander, a little over two years after Asher, I had grown immensely into the woman I was meant to be. The shift in confidence and the shift in personal growth came with my deliverance from many things. I was more intentional in spending time with God, listening to worship music, opening my Bible, and praying. I knew I had certain strongholds to overcome in my life, such as self-doubt, fear, and the need for affirmation. I intentionally prayed over each struggle. I played Lauren Daigle's song "You Say" and Hillsong Worship's song "Who You Say I Am" on repeat. Slowly, I began to see myself through God's truth even more. The aftermath of the show and allowing others to speak into my life for far too many years kept me from discovering my true identity in Christ. When I felt Chris wasn't affirming me in our marriage during this time, I began to write out phrases like "you're strong," "you're worthy," "you're talented," "you're beautiful" on sticky notes and placed them on my bathroom mirror to help lift me up. Chris never lacked in giving affection (although the notes made him give even more), but the lie of needing others' validation to feel complete would leave me feeling empty. Once I began to actively and daily put God first in all things, including my thoughts, I began to take those notes down because I didn't need them anymore. I knew God saw me as all of those things I wanted to believe of myself and so much more. I knew I was loved as I was, because he created me. I no longer needed to strive for anything else.

Once Zander came along, I was juggling a lot more work for my business as well as maintaining the household, but with my newfound identity, I was able to find grace in the everyday. When Zander was still a newborn, I was able to be present and attentive at photo shoots and pop-up shops, even if I had a baby on my hip. That's because I had a confidence in myself as a mother and also a passion to create and make my dreams happen.

Now I give myself grace as a mother and entrepreneur. When the two roles overlap, I do the best I can and know that's enough. If Zander's nap has to happen during a photo shoot and I need to take extra time to get him down, that's okay. Nothing is perfect, but accepting that fact lets me see the blessings woven into the chaos, to be easy on myself, and then to also pass on that same grace to others. Just as Esther was divinely prepared for "such a time as this," so am I.

And so are you.

NINETEEN

FROM BACHELORETTE
TO BOSS

Former Bachelorette Desiree Siegfried is
taking the wedding-gown industry by storm—
all from her Southeast Portland studio.

—*OREGON BRIDE ONLINE*

Perseverance? Check!
Talent? Check!
Willingness to work hard? Check!
Passion? Check, check, and check!
When it comes to the checklist for entrepreneurial success,
I thought I had everything I needed when I set out to make my
dreams a professional reality. I assumed that if I was living out

my passion, then blessings would follow and my life would be fulfilled.

I learned a different lesson.

I've shared that I started a wedding gown line called Desiree Hartsock Bridal, but I haven't gone into detail about the futile, yearlong struggle to make it everything I wanted. Key word: *I*.

• • •

For as long as I can remember, I was drawing clothes and fascinated by sewing. Throughout high school, I always felt misplaced in my standard classes, and when the question "What do you want to be when you grow up" was asked, I would balk and mumble something like, "I dunno, maybe do hair." The Myers-Briggs tests my high school teachers inflicted on me always determined I should be a social worker or something similar. In hindsight, I can see those results correlated to my personality but didn't reflect my interests.

Luckily, in my junior year, I saw a poster in the school's marketing department that advertised the Fashion Institute of Design and Merchandising in Los Angeles, California. One glance at the neon-colored poster with a figure walking down a runway in a trendy outfit and I was sold. I didn't apply to any other school and also didn't want to be anywhere else but California. My entire room during high school was covered in palm tree decor, from my bedspread to my picture frames. I'd proudly purchased the palm tree–themed decor from my meager Outback Steakhouse paycheck (I had to put the items on layaway at Walmart). You know the saying "Dress for the job you want"? Instead of dressing my body, I was dressing my room for the life I wanted!

Little did I know that I was practicing to become an

entrepreneur. I didn't dare let anyone peek inside my sketch-book, but nothing fulfilled me more than my pencil winging its way across a blank sheet of paper or guiding fabric through a whirring sewing machine. I designed and sewed multiple dresses during my senior year. Then I was off to California and fashion school. My dreams of being the next hot thing in fashion were quickly hampered by the cost of Cali living, student debt, and the realization that I had no way of getting experience in the design industry since I couldn't afford to take the precious time to do unpaid internships or even create a pretty portfolio.

As I previously shared, I did catch a break when I got a job as a production assistant at a plus-size women's clothing company before becoming the sole designer for them. It was the best job I could have possibly found to learn the ways of small business and how to take a product from concept to consumer. I would visit our sewing manufacturers, do quality control, choose colors and fabrics, and ultimately design the styles. Overseeing every step of a garment's life was the inspiration I needed to keep my dream alive. And no matter what, I always found my way back to styling brides in bridal salons just so I could be close to the dresses themselves.

Fast-forward to when I started Desiree Hartsock Bridal, after I had Asher. I was a new mom and eager to move forward on the plans I had begun so long ago. To simplify my working mom life, I wanted to make my business procedures as easy as possible. First mistake. Instead of going the route I should've, I decided to design my first collection with a foreign manufacturer because they would be a one-stop shop. I could send them my designs, work through the specs, and choose the laces and materials from their stock. They would manufacture and ship the dresses directly to me. Sounds like a dream come true, right? It certainly did to me, especially as a new mom who was still in the hazy grip of those early newborn months. I said, "Let's do it!"

I got the first shipment of dresses and tore into the huge box. I couldn't wait to see my lifelong design dreams come alive in silk, embroidery, and chiffon. But as I unzipped the garment bags and hung up the dresses, I frowned. Some of the styles hadn't translated the way I had envisioned and sketched them. But I figured I was just getting to know the factory and the way they worked, and that the next collection would turn out better. I didn't want to waste time and money making more samples, so I went ahead with the dresses the factory had sent and launched my first collection.

I couldn't wait for my gowns to be in stores. My expectations were high, and the fears that made me hide my sketchbook as a teen were gone. But it is *extremely* difficult to break out as a new designer in the bridal industry, where high-end, established brands dominate the landscape.

Desiree Hartsock Bridal got to show at Bridal Fashion Week in New York and was picked up by multiple stores. Several of the buyers thought sales were guaranteed based on my celebrity status. This is the downfall of having recognition as a reality TV star. Many people assume your name alone equals cash money, and while it does offer a large audience, many reality TV stars who try to create and run their own companies don't last because their audience sees them through the lens of whatever reality TV show they appeared on, and that doesn't give a lot of leeway for launching a clothing label or a perfume line. Reality stars are known for their personal lives, and if you weren't an "expert" in a category before, then you aren't taken seriously in that arena after fame finds you. For instance, we all love Chip and Joanna Gaines (Who doesn't? The Magnolia Market is basically the Promised Land), but we also know they are experts in the fields of interior design and renovation. If they met on a dating show with no mention of their design skills, we might do a double take if we suddenly saw their home decor book on the shelves at Target.

In my case, the shows included a few clips of my bridal stylist life, but from the fans' point of view, my identity is the Bachelorette, not a designer (despite my having a degree from FIDM and experience as a bridal stylist at several couture salons). Funnily enough, if you look at my résumé, my stints on the shows take up six months, while my fashion-related jobs span more than a decade. However, I have to continually work to change my identity from "Bachelorette" to "designer." It's a journey I will gladly be on until the day my gowns are known for my talent and not only the fact that I've handed out rose boutonnieres on a reality TV show.

One of the problems in the early life of my company was that many of the stores relied solely on my own marketing efforts and my audience. My team and I tried the best we could, but the majority of brides don't purchase a gown based on a designer's name. It is an emotional purchase, and it isn't swayed by the name on the tag inside the dress. I know this firsthand after working with brides for so many years. I always knew my styles weren't going to be for everyone, but the less-than-stellar sales left me humbled.

I stayed extremely busy working on another collection and then another. In apparel, the time it takes to bring a product from concept to manufacturing to retail or consumer can take at least six months to a year. Since I had to work so far in advance, it was difficult to ever slow down or stop to reflect on the decisions I was making. But I felt the Lord tugging on my soul and telling me I needed to follow my own design vision and bring manufacturing to the United States so I could be more hands-on with the production process. Well, I fought this pull every step of the way. Working with my factory had become so easy. I didn't have many overhead expenses and didn't need other employees for that phase of design. I could work last minute (a busy mom's saving grace) and still make things happen.

I let the Lord tug on my soul for months until the pull was too strong to ignore. It was then that I stepped back and realized my own efforts to create the brand I always wanted weren't working. My endless hours trying to raise awareness for my label, get my gowns in additional stores, and increase sales weren't working. Just as I had in my dating life, I was striving and acting on things with my own willpower. For months God had been speaking to me. I would stumble across verses in the Bible containing messages that I knew were from him. They told me I needed to trust his will and stop trying to succeed on my own.

Even when I felt that I got the message and was beginning to make decisions that would lead me to the restructuring of my business, I was drawn to new messages in the Bible telling me to trust God over myself in all areas. I prayed, "God, I feel like I'm listening to what you're saying, and I'm working on getting new production started in the US, so where else in my life am I trusting my own will over yours?"

The more I prayed and continued to work toward a new in-house collection produced locally, along with an online store, the more peace I had over every decision. I turned to God each time a decision came up, and through prayer, he gave me the wisdom to make the right choice. Before, I was stressed to the max, adding to my workload every second without anything to show for it. Now I was working in the presence of God and allowing him to guide my every move. He alone knows where the path goes, but it is in our best interest as his children to trust the path we're on and to look to him for our next steps.

I'm currently creating a customizable collection where a customer will be able to choose the style of top and the style of bottom to ultimately design their own dress. This was a concept I had sketched out over ten years ago. It has always been on my heart but was buried by my worldly desire to "fit in" with trendy new looks. My styles are different from the mainstream bridal look, and I love that about them. They offer effortless comfort to a bride playing the part of a princess. I imagine them as an extension of oneself, not an addition. Forget fussy frills and I-can't-breathe fits—my gowns are easy to wear. My love for the beach and nature is expressed in each design, and that means my dresses are ideal for destination weddings and laid-back gatherings. They are perfect for the bride who wants something different.

Designing my new collection from my ten-year-old vision and bringing manufacturing to the United States have been so empowering. I still am in the middle of making big decisions and transitions for my business, but I strive to seek the Lord for each one to know I'm always in step with his will. I've realized that our desires and our passions can be formed into purpose only when we act on them by faith. Once we listen to what God's will is, then we can know we're headed in the right direction and that the destination will be more fulfilling than we can anticipate.

And that feels pretty dang good.

TWENTY

A HEART OF PURPOSE

Through personal life lessons and glimpses into
my life now, I look forward to sharing how God
has transformed not only my heart but the way I
live each day in faith, with a heart of purpose.

—*ME, IN THE "ABOUT" SECTION OF MY BLOG*

You might think I had enough on my plate with rebranding
my label and creating a new collection, but when we trust
God, he paves the way for *big* things. The road isn't just straight
and clear—it's wide and has room for things we don't expect.

As I brought Desiree Hartsock Bridal under God's will, I felt
another tug on my soul. Nothing was unclear about this tug. God
wanted me to share more about my faith.

It wasn't without risk. I knew that the moment I was open

about my faith on my platforms, I would receive fewer social media collaborations with brands, which made up the majority of the income I put toward my business. It was a risk from not only a personal perspective but also a professional one. However, if I learned anything from my past, it's that whenever an opportunity requires risk or a leap of faith, greater things await.

Putting the financial and personal worries aside, I embarked on creating faith-based content. I would post encouraging messages, verses, and even prayers on my Instagram to start sharing more of my heart for others. Ironically enough, the more I focused on encouraging and uplifting others, the more my own insecurities and struggles diminished.

Then another step became clear. I knew in my heart that God wanted me to start a podcast.

As I often do, I fought this realization for quite some time. Doubts masquerading as concerns plagued me. How would I find the time? Where would I begin? I didn't even listen to podcasts—why on earth would I be good at hosting one? Then came the insecurities. I'm not a pastor or a theologian. I'm not equipped to give messages. I was also downright intimidated. With a podcast, there is no hiding. It's only you, sitting in front of a mic, your voice broadcasting to the world at large. It wouldn't be just a step outside my comfort zone. It would be more like a football field–sized leap outside my comfort zone.

But the more I pushed the idea to the back of my mind, the more it came to the forefront of my thoughts. I would open the Bible and come across stories of the least likely disciples being called to do great things. This all was happening in March 2020, when the world was suddenly faced with COVID-19, lockdowns, closures, and quarantining. It was a time when millions needed encouragement. It was also right when I was beginning the journey of writing this book, which also inspired the podcast.

Again, God's timing is everything.

Even though the thought of a podcast made me want to dry heave into a paper bag, I knew I had to move forward. I didn't have everything figured out. Far from it. But I felt that God was telling me that I didn't have to be perfect before I started talking about him. After all, that's where he comes in—in our weakness and our fear and our doubt. I stepped out in faith, purchased the podcast equipment, and started booking guests. I also named it. It's the *Heart of Purpose* podcast, and the title captures my intent and vision for it. To have a heart of purpose every day is to live in H.O.P.E.

The blessings from the podcast have been astounding. Since the day when I sat down and pushed *Record* on my first episode, I've had the opportunity to interview such inspiring women and carry on those conversations with my listeners after posting the episodes. The discussions have been healing and inspiring for me as I get to hear how God has worked in the lives of both my guests and listeners. In addition, building friendships with like-minded women all over the world through the podcast has filled my soul in ways I can't even express. For me, "fitting in" has always been a struggle. I never felt like anyone truly knew me, or wanted to try. When it comes down to it, I'm an introvert who finds one-on-one conversations far more enjoyable than crowded rooms. I always felt overlooked or misunderstood. God has used this outlet as a tool of connection, and I've found my people— not with the world, not with the TV crowd I'm often associated with, but with women who seek to put God first in all they do, or at least want to learn how to. Through listeners' encouraging messages I am more affirmed than ever to keep pushing through my own insecurities and stand firm in the position God has put before me to bear witness to his love and spread hope. When we allow God to lead in our lives, he uses us in more ways than we could ever imagine.

More than anything, God desires his people to seek him. He wants us to turn from destruction, lies, bitterness, and sin to discover a greater purpose for our lives. Even through writing this book, I've discovered new ways that God has been building my character ever since I was a child, strengthening my spirit in the hurt, and softening my heart in forgiveness. All of this has been to equip me for the greater calling he has in store for me. My relationship with my brother has even been mended as we both continue our spiritual walk with the Lord and understand how the wounds of the past have affected us both. There's just so much beauty and redemption in God's love for us all that no matter what has happened in your life, it can be made new.

Motherhood. Pursuing passions. Faith. I've walked these three parallel paths for some time now, and I'm committed to helping others who find themselves on similar journeys. Looking forward, I'm so excited to keep sharing and growing and inspiring. I know I'm finally in the place God wants for me and that it took the heartaches I experienced as a young girl and my difficult tenure as a reality TV star to find my way here.

Maybe you look around at your life and you find yourself at a crossroads. Or maybe you find yourself lost and aren't certain how you got so far from where you want to be. Or perhaps the road you thought you wanted isn't what you hoped, and you don't know where to go from there. I understand. I've been at those intersections, I've been without a GPS, and I've been searching for the right signs. I can tell you that the roads we find ourselves on often aren't easy. But if we surrender ourselves to God and stand in his truth, we are empowered to let go of road maps that don't make sense for us anymore. Then we see that the roads we travel might be hard, but they make us stronger for having walked them, and in the end, they lead us to who we are truly meant to be.

AUTHOR NOTE

Dear Reader,

As I write this, we are currently living through a pandemic, civil unrest, an economic upheaval, and unfathomable evil and corruption. I can only imagine what our world—and your life—look like right now as you read this. No doubt you have challenges, heartbreak, rejection, and high stakes of your own. Whatever you're facing right now, there are significant truths for you to hear: Beloved, you are seen. You are heard. Your thoughts matter. Your voice matters. More than ever before.

God desires to know you personally. He wants you to come out of that closet where you've been hiding with your pain. He wants to heal your heart and your wounds, to be the father you may never have had, and to be the first one you turn to in the morning and when you lay your head down at night.

If there is anything you can take away from my journey, I

pray it is this: your worth does not lie in the relationship you are in, the number of likes on your social media posts, the amount of money in your bank account, or the status of your job. You are a child of God, uniquely made for a purpose. That is your true identity, and in that truth you are set free. Don't allow the opinions, comparisons, and social pressures to keep you from believing you are loved. Don't follow the crowd as the world sees fit. Follow and listen to the one who sculpted your every intricacy, who knows your past and forgives it all, who hears you in the present and listens, who affirms a hope and a future for you. He is calling out to you to return to him. Will you answer?

Forgive yourself. Forgive those who have wronged you. God's grace is sufficient, and nothing you can do could make him turn away from you. He forgives you.

I pray that hope finds you wherever you are. Whether this pandemic has caused a loss of a job, a loss of a loved one, or the loss of faith, don't give up. There is more to come for you. If I gave up back in high school, I would have never pursued design. If I didn't stay faithful, trusting God's will, I wouldn't have been on the show. If I gave up after Brooks left, I wouldn't have two beautiful boys and a loving husband. If I gave up when my business didn't seem to take off, I wouldn't be able to witness the many brides walking down the aisle in one of my gowns. If I were to have had my bills paid off sooner or a steadier, better paying job, I wouldn't have taken so many risks that ultimately led me here.

Of course, there are thorns and obstacles in each one of our stories, but time and time again, God has shown me that it's those very setbacks and challenges that lead us to the most beautiful roads. Blessings and favor may not come when we want them to, but he provides right on time.

Surrender it all to the Lord and he will guide you. There is no time like today to discover your true worth and identity as beloved by God.

Love to you,
XO, Desiree

DES'S
ACKNOWLEDGMENTS

Now that you have learned more about my entire life, I'm opening the door for you to get a glimpse of the many wonderful friends, family, and people who made this all possible and have stood by me through thick and thin.

When I first sought out to write my story, I didn't know where to begin. Luckily, Autumn Krause, coauthor of this book, became my saving grace. We first met about ten years ago, styling brides together at a Beverly Hills bridal boutique. With her dreams of becoming an author and my dreams of designing on the forefront of our minds, we never could have imagined that we would one day work together on writing this book. Autumn, you are an incredible writer, patient beyond belief with my many close calls to the deadline, and a true blessing. Thank you for the time and care taken to help bring my stories to life.

Of course, I wouldn't have a story to tell without the ones who brought me into this world. Thank you, God! And thanks, Mom and Dad, for always being a steady stream of faithfulness and inspiration that has allowed me to always trust in love.

I wouldn't be able to handle the punches or the pressures that have come, and continue to come, my way without the training from my brother, Nate. You are a true prophet, and while the truth may sting at times, you are one who will always bring it. Thanks for showing me how to be bold and courageous! Lory, you encourage me each and every day with your tenacity and strength. I'm so thankful to be able to call you a sister.

My knight in shining armor, my husband, my chef, and other half, Chris. You're more than I could have ever imagined, and I wouldn't be able to pursue my dreams or do this thing called "parenting" without your patience, support, and steady love. Thank you for saying yes to *The Bachelorette* casting agents and for choosing me each and every day! I love you so much.

Asher and Zander, you inspire me every day to be a better person, to see the world through your eyes and to love others the way you both do, and to be silly and have dance parties at any time of the day. You make my soul happy. Thank you for making me a mother and for the joy you bring into my life!

To all my friends, you know who you are, thank you for all the support and all the grace you all have shown me. You're all in different places across the country, but the sisterhood I feel with each one of you is special and appreciated. I wouldn't have been able to get through many of my lows without you by my side. Even when you may not have known I was in a bad place, you were always there for me, making me laugh, reminding me how life is supposed to be lived: together.

ACKNOWLEDGMENTS

Much of my story—the juicy moments as a reality TV star—would never have happened without the decision-making of the many executives at Warner Bros., ABC, and NZK Productions. Thank you for seeing something in me that I didn't even see in myself at the time and for trusting your gut and allowing me to live out my much-needed story on TV (and off) to bring hope to others through it. A special thanks to Cassie Scalettar and Peter Geist, the producers who were by my side during *The Bachelorette* and had to deal with my many emotional collapses while filming. You two always gave me so much grace and comfort through it all.

Thanks and RIP to the many roses that brought me to my beautiful fate on *The Bachelorette*.

Sarah Morgan, you're my work wife, and I wouldn't have it any other way. We grew in our faith together and continue side by side as we live out our professional dreams. Thanks for taking the reins so many times when I first had both the boys and as I spent time writing this book. I couldn't do it all without you!

The moment Autumn and I got off a call with Keely Boeving, with Wordserve Literary Group, we knew we wanted to have her as the agent for this book. Keely, your soft-spoken yet direct flow of words speaks volumes to your work, and your direction spoke to my love language. Thank you for all you've done to make this book come to life and for being an advocate for our vision.

Stephanie Smith, Bridgette Brooks, Curt Diepenhorst, and the entire team at Zondervan and HarperCollins Publishing, you all are absolutely fantastic to work with. I've known I wanted to write a book for a very long time, but the timing of it all, and the interest you showed, couldn't have been ordained any better. It was a match made in heaven. I adore you all and have to thank you from the bottom of my heart for believing in this book and my story as much as I do. Thanks also for the guidance and direction as we refined each and every word, thought through every marketing plan, and decided on the book cover.

To everyone who has ever listened to a *Heart of Purpose* podcast episode; read this book; liked or commented on one of my posts; or followed, direct messaged, or supported me in any way online or off, I want to say thank you. Putting my life out there for everyone to scrutinize isn't always easy, but the kindness you've shown has paved the way for healing, restoration, encouragement, and inspiration to keep on sharing God's love in every way I can. Thank you!

AUTUMN'S ACKNOWLEDGMENTS

Because I'm a hard-core *Bachelor/Bachelorette* fan, working on this book has been an absolute dream. It didn't feel like work at all, so much as an extended girls' night in which I got to watch old seasons and chat with Des about each episode. All we were missing was wine.

I would like to offer this rose to—I mean, thank—the wonderful staff at Zondervan/HarperCollins for giving this memoir its home. Stephanie Smith, editor extraordinaire, thank you for your expertise and kindness.

Keely Boeving, thank you for being such an amazing advocate and agent. Unlike the *Bachelor/Bachelorette* shows, you made the process drama free (leaving all the good stuff for the book).

Thank you to all my writer friends for always being ready with advice and encouragement. Nikki Barthelmess, thank you for timing my writing sessions and always being just a text away. I love you. Jenn Bishop, Kate Pentecost, Amparo Ortiz, and Aimee Payne—I'm so lucky to have you guys in my corner. And, *of course*, Christianna Marks. Lady, you are simply the best. Expect one thousand copies of this book. See you on the gram. Also to Frankie Munson—you aren't a writer, but I adore you and I love our daily chats, so thank you for being you.

To my family (hai, Kyyy and Lei Lei. Lol, Seth and Dad) and mother-in-law, Kathie, all my thanks, always. None of you watch the *Bachelor/Bachelorette*, but you listened to me talk enthusiastically about it for six months straight.

Thank you to my daughter, Juliet, for being such a bright light in my life and to my son, Declan. You were born right when this book was due, making it the most dramatic season finale of my personal life ever. I love you two so much.

Mark, you earned this acknowledgment for always watching the *Bachelor/Bachelorette* with me. What would I be without you? Ever mine, ever thine, ever ours.

And to Des. Girl, I can't thank you enough for bringing me along on this journey and for letting me help tell your powerful and beautiful story. Yes, it's about your time on the shows, but it's also about so much more, and it's truly moved me. We first met as bridal stylists, yet you saw my love for writing and gave me this opportunity. That's a true friend, and I am so thankful for you. You inspire me in so many ways. You will always be my most favorite Bachelorette.

Finally, to God. Thank you for giving me a love for words and the opportunities to use them. *Omnia Gloria Deo.*

NOTES

1. *Us Weekly*, July 15, 2003.
2. A framed copy of Chris's poem "Hesitations, No More" sits on
   my bedside table to this day. Here it is in its entirety:

Hesitations, No More

At first you aren't sure what to think,
Losing track of those back home . . . not in mind.
Coming into a situation, the unknown,
A skeptic in the present time.

I step out of that limo,
You . . . standing there beautiful in that dress.
I lost my breath for that moment,
Then thought, getting down on one knee would be best.

Time did go by,
The thought of you was all I had.
Until you gave me that chance,
On the dodge ball field . . . I wasn't all that bad.

Then it clicked for me,
I knew on top of that hotel, right then and there,
My feelings for you were building and real,
The skeptic in me to be found, nowhere!

We're dancing, we're talking, I'm thinking about us,
The possibility of you and I no longer imagination for me,
But kissing you and holding you and sharing my life with
     you . . .
A must!

So as you go through this journey,
Along emotional roads not straight, but curvy.
Remember I'm here and I'm thinking of you,
And the thought of us now is ever so true!